RESULTS

the key to continuous school improvement

M I K E   S C H M O K E R

ASSOCIATION FOR SUPERVISION AND CURRICULUM DEVELOPMENT
ALEXANDRIA, VIRGINIA

ASCD

Association for Supervision and Curriculum Development
1250 N. Pitt Street
Alexandria, Virginia 22314
Telephone: 703-549-9110; Fax: 703-299-8631

Printed in the United States of America.

Gene R. Carter, *Executive Director*
Michelle Terry, *Assistant Executive Director, Program Development*
Ronald S. Brandt, *Assistant Executive Director*
Nancy Modrak, *Managing Editor, ASCD Books*
Margaret A. Oosterman, *Associate Editor*
Mary Riendeau, *Project Assistant*
Gary Bloom, *Manager, Design and Production Services*
Karen Monaco, *Designer*
Tracey A. Smith, *Print Production Coordinator*
Cynthia Stock, *Desktop Publisher*

ASCD Stock No. 196017
$16.95
pcr 4/96

Library of Congress Cataloging-in-Publication Data
Schmoker, Michael J.
   Results : the key to continuous school improvement / Mike
Schmoker.
     p. cm.
   Includes bibliographical references and index.
   ISBN 0-87120-260-3 (pbk.)
   1. School improvement programs—United States. 2. Educational change—United States. 3. Education—Aims and objectives—United States. I. Title.
LB2822.82.S35 1996
371.2'00973—dc20   96-4489
                                             CIP

99 98 97 96   4 3 2 1

To Bart and Mary;
and to Cheryl, Michelle, and Megan

The problem is not tests per se but the failure...to be results focused and data driven. Coaches regularly adjust performance in light of ongoing results, even dramatically altering their lesson plans in light of unexpectedly poor results.

—Grant Wiggins

We can, whenever and wherever we choose, successfully teach all children whose schooling is of interest to us.

—Ron Edmonds

Results: The Key to Continuous School Improvement

Foreword   vii

Introduction   1

1   Teamwork   9

2   Goals   17

3   Performance Data   29

4   Rapid Results: The Breakthrough Strategy   49

5   Research   65

6   Redefining Results   69

7   Opportunities for Action Within and Among
    the Subject Areas   81

Conclusion: Leadership   103

Appendix   109

References   111

Index   118

About the Author

Mike Schmoker is Research Analyst for the Amphitheater Public Schools in Tucson, Arizona, where he works with teachers and administrators to promote and facilitate continuous improvement. He has studied and visited numerous schools and districts that demonstrate the effective use of continuous improvement principles. With Richard Wilson, he is coauthor of *Total Quality Education: Profiles of Schools That Demonstrate the Power of Deming's Management Principles,* published by Phi Delta Kappa.

You can reach him at Amphitheater Public Schools, 701 West Wetmore Road, Tucson, Arizona 85705. Telephone: 520-690-7796.

Foreword

I am heartened every day by what I see in schools and classrooms throughout the United States and around the world. There are many educational environments in which teachers are coaching learners to think at higher levels, to master competencies that stretch and broaden the edges of possibilities, and to connect their learning to meaningful entities. We have launched numerous initiatives for improving the delivery of curriculums; spent untold hours in creating visions, missions, and goals; and captured the true spirit of what it means to be site based in our decision making. Despite these diligent efforts, we are perceived as falling far short of the expectations of the public, the business community, legislators, and even ourselves in preparing all students for productive citizenship and work-force successes that will result in an improved economy. What then is the next step in showing ourselves approved in producing an entire planet of young people who can use their own wit and imagination to solve problems, address complex issues that invade contemporary societies, and create solutions by using a repertoire of knowledge from various contexts?

Mike Schmoker proposes a solution to the age-old dilemma of having every learner achieve at higher levels and make productive entries into the world of work. He declares that all school efforts should be focused on results. He insists that all schools can improve if they gear up to get better results by examining and refining the processes that most clearly contribute to designated results. Attention to increased standards and appropriate measures of their attainment are key factors in his remedy for poor performance.

The human cry has been to raise standards. Perhaps the first step is to determine what these standards should be. An inquiry to determine the skills and knowledge needed to function in today's technological, information-based society must be examined and compared to what students are learning in schools. Once established viii

as thrusts of rigor and relevance, the standards must be malleable with time and new research.

To get desired results, there must be assessments based on the standards. Without connectivity of the two, we are like sailors trying to sail without a wind, hoping that we end up at the desired port. Students in the United States have the most content requirements in the world, but most testing does not require them to apply their theoretical knowledge of a subject to real-world situations. Assessments based on content requirements that are not connected to demonstration is much like a sterile financial audit where only one correct response is acceptable. For an assessment system to have comprehensive results, it must teach students and teachers rather than just measure bits and pieces of knowledge out of usable context.

The public microscope on education is being focused to the highest power. Getting results means more than increased scores on standardized tests and the lauding of the number of students admitted to ivy league colleges. Getting results means that all learners are provided with relevant, mind-enhancing experiences that can be demonstrated through assessment frameworks requiring evidence of thought.

—FRANCES FAIRCLOTH JONES
ASCD President, 1996–97

Introduction

Schools, classrooms, and school systems can and do improve, and the factors facilitating improvement are neither so exotic, unusual, or expensive that they are beyond the grasp of...ordinary schools.

—Clark, Lotto, and Astuto 1984

The annual goal statements that emerge from school improvement efforts are rarely linked to student achievement, and they seldom challenge the basic elements of practice.

—McGonagill 1992

School improvement is not a mystery. Incremental, even dramatic, improvement is not only possible but probable under the right conditions. The purpose of this book is to elaborate on the simple conditions that favor results, briefly discuss the theory behind the conditions, and demonstrate, using examples from schools, how anyone in virtually any school setting can begin to successfully replicate these conditions.

A recurrent theme is an emphasis on principles and practices that (1) are simple and supported by research, (2) are relatively few in number, and (3) have huge but underused potential. Consider only this—school goals are "rarely linked to student achievement" (McGonagill 1992). We don't need to look any further for why the school improvement movement, for all the knowledge it has generated and passion it has aroused, is moving forward at such a relatively slow pace. Perhaps this is a function of what Fullan and Miles (1992) write in an examination of school reform:

> Reform often fails because politics often favors symbols over substance. Substantial change in practice requires a lot of hard and clever work "on the ground," which is not the strong point of political players (p. 746).

Our concern with politics has caused us to overlook the most obvious on-the-ground concerns about our real purposes—our goals.

1

2   We have launched initiatives (e.g., site-based management), provided loads of staff development in certain methods (e.g., "Essential
Elements of Instruction"), and spent untold hours drawing up visions
and mission statements. All had enormous promise. But these sym-
bolic, high-profile "initiatives du jour" occurred in the near absence
of any written or explicit intention to monitor, adjust, and thus
palpably increase student learning or achievement. The combination
of three concepts constitutes the foundation for results: meaningful
teamwork; clear, measurable goals; and the regular collection and
analysis of performance data. Chapters 1–3 describe these results and
explore the three concepts, which have a remarkable potential for
transforming almost any school or district.

In this era of heightened interest in school reform, we have yet
to realize that organizations typically get what they earnestly and
specifically set out to get. Good-faith efforts to establish goals and
then to collectively and regularly monitor and adjust actions toward
them produce results.

We have to acknowledge that people work more effectively,
efficiently, and persistently when they work collectively, while gauging their efforts against results (Rosenholtz 1991). Results goad, guide,
and motivate groups and individuals. Experience by itself does not
adequately inform us on the quality of education we are providing.
It typically thwarts innovation (Little 1990), tending to encourage
teachers and administrators to carry out activities as they always have,
regardless of whether an activity's effectiveness can be demonstrated.

Twenty-six years ago, John Goodlad (Goodlad, Klein, and Associates 1970) told us that even "innovation" is not enough, that
"behind the classroom door," even teachers who think they are
implementing an innovation are often only "twisting" it right back
into what they have always done (p. 72). We have been naive;
without the reference point that results provide, experience is often
a slow and misleading teacher. Informed changes in practice can
produce timely, even rapid, incremental advances. Ways to promote
such steady and rapid improvement do exist. They are the subject of
Chapter 4.

Overreliance on first-person experience prevents improvement
and keeps educators from seeking other information sources, such as
effective, formal research on best practices or their consequences
(Little 1990). Such activity is unfortunate, considering the rich legacy
of what we have learned in the last 30 years about how to improve
schools, districts, and classroom instruction. We have not come close
to taking advantage of this knowledge. I explore this issue throughout
the book, especially in Chapter 5.

My aim is to spotlight a handful of essential concepts that others
have developed but that perhaps have not received sufficient atten-

tion where they matter most—in classrooms and schools. Much of the best that we know has been lost in the mass of information and issues that have competed for the spotlight for over 10 years. In this chaos, we remembered "reform" and "restructuring" in all their bewildering manifestations. But we may have inadvertently overlooked what is both the cause and effect of school improvement—concrete improvement itself. The principles and schools that are cited can provide a good beginning. If we wish to move more effectively from means to ends, we must do a better job of "connecting the dots."

Education literature contains numerous references to results. But results have rarely become operational. And, as I try to show, schools have an almost cultural and ingrained aversion to reckoning with, much less living by, results. A deep and debilitating confusion about how means relate to ends has always been one of the marks of the teaching profession (Lortie 1975, Sizer 1992).

The word "results" may even seem troublesome. It has been dragged in and out of many contexts, sounding sensible one moment, retrograde the next. We are sometimes uneasy about its use: "Results" is heard infrequently at school and district planning sessions. Some reject it for representing an implicit disregard for "process." For others, it carries the unspoken implication that results must be obtained at any cost or at the expense of what is truly best for children.

Concepts that seem to have been borrowed from business are often misunderstood. They are made to bear the burden of every sinister possibility, raising fears of a ruthless and mechanistic perversion of schooling that will supplant the best that schools now do. Looking for results may even smack of the worst kind of accountability: an exclusive insistence on raising test scores.

"Results" does not have such a narrow meaning in this book. Chapters 6 and 7 suggest how we can move beyond a limited view of achievement to one that embraces both standardized testing as well as the exciting recent advances in alternative assessment. Results should be understood as a thoughtfully established, desired end-product, as evidence that something worked (or did not work). In this sense, all results—good or bad—are ultimately good, because they provide feedback that can guide us, telling us *what to do next* and how to do it better. Feedback, then, is synonymous with results. And though results have some connection to accountability, that connection is only one dimension of its importance.

An emphasis on results is central to school improvement. We are seeing that such improvement undeniably affects the lives of children, what they earn, and what they become (Bishop 1995). This effect cannot be taken for granted. We do not give results the central concern they deserve; thus, we have neglected the actions and

4

attitudes that will help us get better results. We talk as though we want results, but we generally fail to make the kind of systematic, organized effort that produces them. The principles I examine are intended to close the gap between intent and successful "on-the-ground" effort toward improvement.

Concentrating on results does not negate the importance of process. On the contrary, the two are interdependent: Results tell us which processes are most effective and *to what extent* and where processes need reexamining and adjusting. Processes exist for results—and results should inform processes. We cannot afford to emphasize one over the other. "We fail," writes Wiggins, to "regularly adjust performance in light of ongoing results" (1994a, p. 18).

A virulent reaction against emphasizing results has occurred in unlikely places. Some of those involved in the Total Quality Management (TQM) movement are uneasy about such a focus. There are reasons for this concern: Many in business are justifiably wary of what happens when the wrong kinds of results govern us. A frequently cited example is quarterly profits, which can compromise long-term growth and quality.

To avoid this pitfall, educators need to be thoughtful and discriminating, taking the lead in defining—and redefining—results. Teachers need to look at student ability to write effectively, read critically, retain information, perform, present, apply, calculate, and analyze. Schools can evaluate these activities and the processes that inform them immediately, within and increasingly among the disciplines (see Chapters 6 and 7). Thoughtlessly rejecting a focus on results should be resisted. Unfortunately, schools typically have been guilty of shorting both processes and results, focusing on one or the other—seldom on both.

The average school still "puts its faith in process, not in results" (Fiske 1992, p. 116). Kevin Castner, former assistant superintendent of schools in Frederick County, Maryland, refers to our "disease of being accountable only for process and procedures" (Bullard and Taylor 1993, p. 80). Educators need to reconceptualize how processes and results interact and refine processes both before and during implementation. Emphasizing only one major or untested process, without careful and frequent analysis, can be disastrous. An example is when the New York City schools poured $120 million into a single process, guidance services, which had never been tested against results. Four years later, schools found that the process did not affect their goal—to reduce the dropout rate. They later discovered the real problem: They needed to make teaching "more appealing to students" (Fiske 1992, p. 64).

Similarly, we implement a range of elaborate processes—such as site-based management, cooperative learning, and whole language instruction—without adequately monitoring the impact. These changes are deep. Regular monitoring, followed by adjustment, is the only way to expect success. History has demonstrated that translating theory into practice, though important, is not enough. We also need an ongoing concern with the real impact we are having. Otherwise, after all our training and fanfare, even the most promising innovations often dissipate into insignificance, as we have seen happen with so many potentially beneficial programs (e.g., the middle school concept, which emphasized active learning methods [Lounsbury and Clark 1990, Gitlin 1990]). As I heard Grant Wiggins say at a recent conference, schools never "pilot" new programs or processes; we just send them off and then "wave at them from the pier, never to be seen again."

A concern with results can remedy this lack without forcing us into the mistakes or excesses of the past. Processes and results are cooperative. The problem is failing to concern ourselves with carefully selected results—and a more precise understanding of which processes most favor them.

Results: The Key to Quality and Improvement

A remarkable finding has emerged about the TQM organizations that succeed: They are concerned with processes only insofar as *these processes affect results* (Brigham 1994). In addition, they are concerned with short-term as well as long-range results. Short-term results act as vital feedback and provide encouragement and momentum toward continued improvement (Schaffer and Thomson 1992).

Employees at the Toyota plant in Georgetown, Kentucky, are concerned with such results as the percentage (measured by tenths of a percentage) of car hoods that fit perfectly in place. In another case, the results of introducing a new conveyor hook into the process were measured by the number of times a part fell off the hook and into a water bath. The plant concentrates on measurable results, such as reliability and repair records, the percentage of cars arriving on the lot in perfect condition, and customer satisfaction data. Processes are always "in the rough"; concern with results ensures that all *processes* are perpetually scrutinized for adjustments. The results at places like Toyota, as well as the schools and organizations this book examines, are intimately connected to processes.

What About Outcomes?

An honest look at schools, districts, and classrooms shows a tenuous relationship between processes and results. What makes this observation surprising is that we are several years into what has been

6   known as the outcome-based movement, the ostensible intent of which is to bring educational results into sharper focus, to finally shed an absorption with inputs in favor of, well, results. The movement did not turn out that way. Why? Because, for all the good that this movement has done in helping us examine and define educational outcomes, it subtly lost its concern with continuous, information-based improvement. Among so-called outcome-based schools and districts, one can rarely find any systematic means to analyze outputs against instruction and inputs. An *Educational Leadership* article reveals that in spite of all the time, talk, and conferences attended, only a handful of districts show any real educational benefits from the outcome-based movement. Johnson City schools— clearly a results-oriented district—come to mind. But they are the exception. Research documenting the effects of outcome-based teaching is still relatively rare: "Testimonials, speeches, and narrative descriptions may be inspirational and helpful, but they provide little solid ground on which to build a reform movement" (Evans and King 1994, p. 12). This movement was heralded as "the greatest reform of all," because it would put an end to our addiction to change for change's sake.

The current ferment about outcome-based education (OBE) does not erase the fact that we all *want better outcomes*. The best aspects of the outcome-based movement had—and still have—an excellent chance of bringing us around to the business of striving for and getting better results. That it has not should alert us to a tendency in schools to avert the confrontation that is at the heart of a true results orientation.

Time for a Breakthrough

We have avoided the difficult though promising task of analyzing what we are doing against the results we are getting. We have learned much about assessment, criteria, and rubrics; brain theory; and ways to make learning more active and engaging. Educational research has given us what systems theorist Peter Senge considers to be the most profound set of discoveries in U.S. history. With all this knowledge, we are dancing on the edge of a revolution in the quality of education we can provide, and arguably, our quality of life. Yet, most schools still do not (1) conscientiously examine the number of students who can do such activities as problem-solve, analyze, calculate, and compose and then (2) adjust instruction accordingly.

Academic outcomes, however, are not the only meaningful results. As Chapters 6 and 7 show, we must also attend to other, closely connected results that are important and clearly influence the learning results we get with our children. Properly selected, such results directly contribute to learning.

Educators can benefit substantially from emphasizing both short-term and long-term results. Incremental, measurable improvement not only can but must occur quickly. But speed does not exclude the need for careful and patient planning to bring about systemwide change. Long-term, system-transforming change relies on "immediate successes," which are "essential if people are to increase their confidence and expand their vision of what is possible" (Schaffer 1988, p. 60). Success breeds success; Schaffer calls this action-oriented effort the "breakthrough strategy" (see Chapter 4). It accounts for the difference between vision that is realized and vision that only exists on paper. As many have discovered, this strategy explains the success of most successful continuous improvement efforts in industry. We educators ignore this principle at great cost.

Properly understood, a concern with results can promote balanced and sensible action that produces higher achievement on a wide range of assessments. I hope to demonstrate this in the following pages. The following assumptions are the basis for my discussion:

- Though a thorough, long-term, cultural transformation should always be the goal of all reform efforts, it must rely on short-term, measurable successes. These successes will result in cultural change and embody change's most important feature—a radical reorientation toward results.

- We are not operating near our potential. Evidence that schools are grossly underperforming organizations surrounds us. Part of the problem is that schools are not true "organizations" (Donahoe 1993).

- Teachers, like other professionals, perform more effectively—even exponentially—if they collaborate. Although collaboration represents a significant change in how most teachers work, it should become an expectation.

- Evidence shows that schools can and will improve if they gear up to strive for increasingly better results by examining and refining the processes that most directly contribute to designated results.

The Highest Stakes

Education has a significant and enduring effect on the students and children who populate our urban, rural, and suburban schools. Preschool programs, good schools, and even "raw" (i.e., excluding other factors) years of education make real differences in people's lives and correlate strongly to the future success of our children and to prosocial, community-building adult behavior—to "changed

8   lives," even among low socioeconomic populations (Berrueta-Clement 1984, Reich 1992). In cognitive areas, effective schools have been found to be more important than background—as much as 6 times more important in reading; 10 times in math (Mortimore and Sammons 1987). A report on education and the economy indicates that "educational attainment is the single most important determinant of a person's success in the labor market.... In the 50 years it has been tracked, the payoff to schooling has never been higher" (Bishop 1995, p. 21). Projections are that demand for the well educated—in number and proportion—will increase and that student payoff will escalate as we enter the 21st century (Bishop 1995).

Can we rise to the occasion? We have already begun. Consider the following results:

• In 1982, none of the students at New York City's Key School could pass the New York City proficiency test in writing. The teachers took deliberate steps to improve students' writing. The following year, 80 percent passed (Hodges 1987).

• The Texas Scholars Program set out to increase the proportion of students taking challenging high school courses. They brought in business professionals to speak at assemblies and to emphasize the workplace importance of succeeding in higher math, chemistry, and physics. Enrollment in these courses doubled and tripled in many cases (Folzenlogen 1993).

• In 1994, an inner-city high school in Poughkeepsie, New York, reached its ultimate goal: to make sure every student attended college. As a result, all 160 of its graduating seniors are headed for college (*Arizona Daily Star* 1994).

Such results are not dry statistics. We cannot dismiss the impact of these triumphs on human lives, on real children. The ultimate result of such efforts is the life- and community-transforming power that an excellent education bestows on students. We cannot afford to overlook the rich opportunity that schools have to make a difference.

As the many schools described in this book demonstrate, there is every reason to believe that we can begin providing a better education for all students, of every class, starting now. We can do it by focusing, unwaveringly, on better results and the conditions that promote them.

1

Teamwork

Teams get results.

—Katzenbach and Smith 1993

In Chapters 1–3, I examine the key components that favor results and improvement: teamwork, goals, and the selective and judicious use of data. Individually, they have limited impact; combined, they constitute a powerful force for improvement—without necessarily consuming large amounts of time or money (though, if properly spent, more of each is always desired). Together, these elements cannot help but promote better results in any context. The many school examples in these pages attest to this concept.

Success depends on the interdependency between collaboration and goals; between both of these and purpose. Though teamwork is fundamental in this scheme, it is "the means, not the end" (Katzenbach and Smith 1993, p. 12). Similarly, Huberman says that collegiality is not a "legitimate end in itself unless it can be shown to affect...the nature or degree of pupil development" (Huberman, in Fullan 1991, p. 136). Chapter 1 defines and discusses the importance and interdependence of effective team collaboration, goals, and data, essential yet often misunderstood issues.

Teacher Isolation

When Thomas Edison was asked why he was so prolific an inventor, he replied that it was a result of what he called the "multiplier effect." He placed his team of inventors near each other to encourage them to consult with one another so that each member of the team benefitted from the collective intelligence of the group. His teams not only worked better but faster (Smith 1985).

We must acknowledge that regardless of the difficulties or the tradition of teacher isolation and the structures that promote it, schools would perform better if teachers worked in focused, supportive teams:

10

Collegiality among teachers, as measured by the frequency of communication, mutual support, help, etc., was a strong indicator of implementation success. Virtually every research study on the topic has found this to be the case (Fullan 1991, p. 132).

Unfortunately, teacher isolation—the opposite of teamwork—is one of the most obvious realities of a teacher's life (Lortie 1975). Lortie saw the negative effects of this isolation: "Teacher individualism is not cocky and self-assured; it is hesitant and uneasy" (p. 210). Such isolation promotes professional insecurity. Many teachers, comfortable in their isolation, may find the transition to teamwork a little daunting. But the teachers Lortie (1975) interviewed were wise enough to know that the limited, hermetically sealed world of the classrooms they inhabited did not favor their growth or a sense of confidence that they were doing a job well. Why? Because, as he discovered,

> Individualism combines with presentism to retard the search for occupational knowledge. Teachers who work in isolation cannot create an empirically grounded, semantically potent common language. Unless they develop terms to indicate specific events, discussion will lack the clarity it needs to enlighten practice....Individualism supports presentism by inhibiting work with others in a search for common solutions. Teachers do not undertake the collegial effort which has played so crucial a role in other occupations (p. 212).

This passage is worth rereading. The first point it makes is that teachers, the front line in the battle for school improvement, are working in isolated environments that cut the lifeline of useful information. Such isolation thwarts them in developing common solutions through dialogue. Isolation tacitly assumes that practitioners have nothing to learn from each other. When I look back on when I taught English, nothing is more apparent to me than experience, by itself, was not the best teacher. And I had virtually no opportunity to learn from my colleagues. We did come together for periodic department meetings, but that type of gathering is not what is meant here by collaboration or teamwork.

The crush of what Lortie calls "presentism"—of myriad daily events and duties—kept us from reflecting collaboratively on such obvious and challenging concerns as how to teach composition more effectively, how to conduct discussions about literature more effectively, and how to make literature exciting. We did not know if or how anyone was teaching composition—or even what that meant. So we worked, consciously or unconsciously, toward our own goals, within the limitations of what each of us knew and did not know. Day-to-day concerns kept us from reflecting on what our most important goals should be.

The absence of a common focus and, by extension, common solutions, can be explained by the absence of what Goodlad (Goodlad et al. 1970) calls clear-cut, specific goals for school at all levels of responsibility. These kinds of goals can only be obtained when professionals regularly collaborate and communicate in an effort to define and reach such goals.

But today, an irrational and indefensible isolation continues to prevent professionals from learning from each other. The bottom line is what kids continue to miss out on as a result.

Isolation is unique to the teaching profession and, by implication, to the whole educational system (Lortie 1975). This observation should shock us, as it did Donald Peterson (1991), former president of Ford Motor Company; Peterson was dismayed by the isolation in which teachers work. A number of circumstances account for this situation: "the organization of space, time, and task seriously constrains interactions" (Little 1990, p. 514); and "the traditional school organization minimizes collective, collegial behavior" (Donahoe 1993, p. 299).

Because so much inhibits work-related teacher interaction, we might be persuaded to believe that this problem is insurmountable. Not so, as the teacher teams highlighted in this book demonstrate. Everyone in the educational community must work diligently to change the structures that impede teamwork. But meanwhile, we must take advantage of the opportunities that already present themselves—and which others have demonstrated can eventuate in better results.

Benefits

Teachers at Donaldson Elementary School in our district were reluctant to spend large chunks of their early-out times in meetings supposedly intended to promote "continuous improvement." But when they began to see collective progress, a direct result of their focused collaboration, the meetings became more meaningful. A good example is what happened when we discussed a key weakness in 2nd grade writing: students' difficulty in writing descriptive settings. After the team brainstormed, a team member proposed having students first draw then describe in writing the setting they imagined for their stories. The number of students able to write high-quality descriptions went from just a few to almost the entire 2nd grade class.

12   Evidence for the benefits of collaboration, rightly conducted, are overwhelming. The nature of the complex work of teaching "cannot be accomplished by even the most knowledgeable individuals working alone" (Little 1990, p. 520). In the typical school, however, teacher practice is "limited to the boundaries of their own experience," without any outside scrutiny or objective analysis. Such boundaries introduce a "conservative bias," which is the enemy of risk and innovation and a recipe for perpetuating the status quo at a time when change is manifestly necessary (Little 1990, pp. 526–527). Little found a strong relationship between the right kind of collegiality and improvements for both teachers and students:

- Remarkable gains in achievement.
- Higher-quality solutions to problems.
- Increased confidence among all school community members.
- Teachers' ability to support one another's strengths and to accommodate weaknesses.
- The ability to examine and test new ideas, methods, and materials.
- More systematic assistance to beginning teachers.
- An expanded pool of ideas, materials, and methods.

Little also quotes Lortie to make the point that the prevailing isolation in which teachers work does little to "add to the intellectual capital of the profession" (Lortie, in Little 1987, pp. 501–502). In the business of teaching and school improvement, intellectual capital—ideas, fresh solutions, and effective teaching methods—is the most precious commodity.

Business literature from theorists such as Tom Peters and W. Edwards Deming is equally as emphatic about how teamwork benefits intellectual and professional capital. For Deming, "there is no substitute for teamwork"; without it, "dissipation of knowledge and effort, results far from optimum," exists (1986, p. 19).

An excellent resource for this topic is *The Wisdom of Teams* (1993) by Jon Katzenbach and Douglas Smith. Their study of teams in 47 organizations corroborates educational studies by educators like Judith Little and Michael Huberman. "It is obvious that teams outperform individuals," that "learning not only occurs in teams but endures" (Katzenbach and Smith 1993, p. 5). Teams "bring together complementary skills and experiences that, by definition, exceed those of any individual on the team...bringing multiple capabilities to bear on difficult issues" (Katzenbach and Smith 1993, pp. 18–19).

Teamwork is perhaps the most effective form of staff development. Two 1st grade teachers at Prince Elementary School in our district have been getting exceptional results for years with students from one of our least advantaged areas, many of whom arrive with very limited skills. What they have learned from each other has enabled them to ensure that an exceptional percentage of their students leaves 1st grade able to read and write on grade level.

Collaboration works. And it also addresses an essential social dimension of improvement. Successfully implementing innovative procedures "is very much a social process" (Fullan 1991, p. 84). Consider, too, the advantages of a focused, interactive culture where work is characterized by a sense of fun, or "joy" in Deming's lexicon. Studies show that people who are members of effective teams "consistently and without prompting emphasized the fun aspects of their work together" (Katzenbach and Smith 1993, p. 19).

I was struck by this same spirit in dozens of workers from the Toyota plant in Kentucky. When I visited them, miles away from their employment, an ex-jockey told me that on Sunday evenings, he "couldn't wait to get with his team to hit the ground running on Monday mornings." Meaningful, purposeful collaboration addresses the social and emotional demands of teaching (Little 1990). And we should not underestimate the social significance of Little's observation that effective collaboration creates that rare arena in which teachers can receive credit and praise for their "knowledge, skill, and judgement" (pp. 18–19). Teamwork provides opportunities to enjoy the social and psychic satisfactions of collective effort.

The Dark Side of Collegiality

In the face of all this evidence, why do we persist in denying these benefits to the profession? The explanation can be found in our failure to be results oriented. Industry is littered with stories about "quality circles" that came and went. Why? Few realized any palpable results, and so they were regarded as a waste of time—the kiss of death for any innovation. Similarly, many teachers find their first attempts at collaboration clumsy and unrewarding. Subsequently, the time they spend in meetings appears to take away from lesson planning and instruction. Predictably, "unproductive" meetings are abandoned (Little 1987, p. 493).

Unproductive, unrewarding meetings—we have all been to them. And because of these experiences, many people simply do not believe that teams perform better than individuals. Katzenbach and Smith (1993) saw how "members waste time in unproductive discussions, which cause more trouble than they are worth...and actually generate more complaints than constructive results" (p. 20). They regard this problem as a lack of discipline and disciplined action, which embodies the essential conditions that favor productive collaboration.

14   We must clearly distinguish between effective collaboration and the appearance of teamwork. We can begin by stating what teamwork, for the purposes of this book, is not. "The term collegiality has remained conceptually amorphous....Much that passes for collegiality does not add up to much" (Little 1990, p. 509). Similarly, the word teamwork "courts imprecision" (Katzenbach and Smith 1993, p. 19). Much of what we call teamwork or collegiality does not favor nor make explicit what *should* be its end: better results for children. The unfortunate reality is that most of what goes on in the name of collegiality is ineffective or counterproductive. "Most alliances among teachers" are not task oriented at all. Instead, they "appear to be informal, voluntary, and distant from the real work in and of the classroom" (Little 1987, p. 507.) This kind of collegiality not only consumes valuable time but can also promote the consequences of isolation that we deplore:

> I argue that the most common configurations of teacher-to-teacher interaction may do more to bolster isolation than to diminish it; the culture that Lortie described as individualistic, present oriented, and conservative is thus not altered but is indeed perpetuated by the most prevalent examples of teacher collaboration and exchange (Little 1990, p. 511).

Alas, the weaker, more common forms of collegiality "serve only to confirm present practice without evaluating its worth." Collegiality may "supply sympathy of the sort that dissuades teachers from the kind of closer analysis of practice that might yield solutions to recurrent problems" and thus accounts for continuing practices that are its ostensible enemy (Little 1990, p. 517). Less formal kinds of collegiality accommodate, even promote, the course of least resistance. This characteristic is part of the "dark side" of collegiality (Fullan 1991, p. 131).

The "bright side" (if you will) is found less frequently. It is rooted in a concern with results, with what Little calls "joint work" that affects gains and classroom performance and involves monitoring student progress and the "thoughtful, explicit examination of practices and their consequences" (Little 1990, p. 519). Huberman writes that collegiality "is not a fully legitimate end in itself, unless it can be shown to affect...the nature or degree of pupil development" (Huberman, in Fullan 1991, p. 136).

The bright side of collegiality can be found at Northview Elementary School in Manhattan, Kansas. Students realized huge gains between 1983 and 1989, when teachers began to collaborate. In reading, 4th and 6th grade scores on district achievement tests rose from 59 to 100 percent, and from 41 to 97 percent, respectively. In math, 4th grade scores rose from 70 to 100 percent; 6th grade scores, from 31 to 97 percent. How? Principal Dan Yunk began to arrange for teams of teachers to meet routinely to analyze scores, identify strengths and weaknesses, and develop ways to effectively address them (Schmoker and Wilson 1993). Something powerful happens when teachers begin to regularly discuss instructional challenges and their solutions.

Teamwork and Data

Teams in our district have begun to brainstorm for solutions to student problems they have identified by using data. A team from Holaway Elementary School used data to determine that the highest area of difficulty in solving multistep math problems was students' ability to write out the steps that led to math solutions. The team then generated possible strategies:

- Provide students with good examples and models of what the writing should look like.
- Ask students to write each step as they complete it, rather than write the entire problem after they have completed the problem.
- Share the writing rubric more explicitly with the students; give them copies.
- Ask students to start their explanation for each step with the phrase, "I did this because."
- Require that students self-assess their work against a specific rubric before they hand in their work.

These ideas were among others that the team generated during only seven minutes of brainstorming (the entire meeting took only about 30 minutes; see Appendix for how to conduct effective meetings). Implementing these ideas brought the team closer to its improvement goal by the next month. Such activity generates "intellectual capital," and by not tapping into it, we deny teachers and students a precious and essential resource in helping greater numbers of students receive a higher-quality education.

A good example attesting to the power of teamwork, clear goals, and data analysis is Adlai E. Stevenson High School in Lincolnshire, Illinois. Teachers work in department teams that conduct ongoing analyses of performance data. Superintendent Richard DuFour said that each team meets once a month to collaborate. They analyze results at least four times a year, and the times are built into the calendar. Nine times a year, students come to school at 10:30 a.m. to give teachers time to collaborate. Many schools have benefitted from

16   such late-ins and early-outs, which have been incorporated into school schedules across the United States.

At Stevenson High School, what happened when time was provided for results-oriented teamwork? In 1985, before the process was introduced, the school did not rank in the top 50 schools in the 13-state Midwest region. In 1992, when goals were established and collaborative time was instituted:

> The school ranked first in the region, and by 1994, it was among the top 20 schools in the world....Last year, the school established new records in every traditional indicator of student achievement, including grade distributions, failure rates, average ACT scores, average SAT scores, percentage of honor grades on Advanced Placement examinations, and average scores in each of the five areas of the state achievement test (DuFour 1995, p. 35).

* * *

Evidence abounds that we can do far more by working as teams in a focused, problem-solving fashion than by working in isolation—real children, real students, benefit immensely. The best news, and this theme is repeated throughout the book, is that the near-absence of powerful elements such as teamwork is in one sense something to celebrate. Even reasonable attempts to increase it can inevitably promote better results.

Good teamwork among grade-level, department, school, and ad hoc teams will give us results we once only dreamed of. Chapter 2 defines the most salient feature of good teamwork, or the "serious collaboration," which Little found to be so rare (1987, p. 513). We have already touched on it: the importance of clear, specific performance goals.

Goals

We did not find a single case in the literature where student learning increased but had not been a central goal.

—Joyce, Wolf, and Calhoun 1993

The goal makes the team.

—Mark Rolewski, Principal, Nash Elementary School

Goals give teamwork meaning. Gene Maeroff (1993) writes that "teams are vehicles for increasing efficiency, effectiveness, and motivation." But what motivates and energizes effective teams? According to Maeroff, the answer is (1) "a clear, elevating goal and (2) a results-driven structure," pointing once again to the interdependency between teamwork and tangible improvement (pp. 514–515). Noel Farmer, superintendent of Frederick County Public Schools in Frederick, Maryland, discusses the importance of goals:

> If you make the goals clear, inviting and doable, attainable, then the goals themselves will drive you, they really drive you. Teachers and principals that buy into it...the doability of it and the clearness of it, they eventually get to the point where they say, "Hey what's happening here? I'm in a whole new ball game." And you see now that people are finding it very rewarding (Farmer, in Bullard and Taylor 1993, p. 123).

Frederick County schools have been very clear about their goals. The school district has gone from the middle of the pack among Maryland school districts to being first or second in every academic category. During a three-year period, Chapter I students went from 2 to 70 percent on grade level. These dramatic improvements occurred in a district known for emphasizing authentic learning activities and assessment. With these results in hand, the district took the unprecedented step of asking the community to raise taxes expressly for raising teachers' salaries. The community agreed.

18   Goals drive us. Psychologist Mihalyi Csikszentmihalyi (1990) has made one of the most interesting discoveries in recent times about the connection between goals and happiness: Goals are the stuff of motivation, persistence, and well-being. In language that echoes Farmer's thoughts, he discovered that generally what people enjoy most is pursuing a clear, doable goal that they value. This connection accounts for why many people are as happy or happier at work than at leisure. In the absence of goals, entropy and aimlessness rush in.

Unfortunately, most schools do not make the connection between goals, motivation, and improvement. We have what is perhaps the most striking, contradictory, self-defeating characteristic of schooling and our efforts to improve it: the gap between the need—and intent—to improve academic performance in our schools on the one hand, and the conspicuous and virtual absence of clear, concrete academic goals in most school or district planning efforts on the other. Without explicit learning goals, we are simply not set up and organized for improvement, for results. Only such goals will allow us to analyze, monitor, and adjust practice toward improvement.

Goodlad (Goodlad et al. 1970) lamented the absence of key reforms that we might reasonably expect to find in our schools and school systems. One of them, already acknowledged for decades, is the necessity of "clearly discernible...clear-cut specified goals for schooling at all levels of responsibility" (pp. 12–13). We are still waiting. The lack of clear goals may provide the most credible explanation for why we are still only "inching along" in our effort to improve schooling for U.S. children (Maeroff 1994, p. 52), for why the results of more than 10 years of reform have been so disappointing (Astuto, Clark, Read, McGree, de Koven, and Fernandez 1994). Rosenholtz (1991) wrote that clear, measurable goals are the "center to the mystery of school's success, mediocrity, or failure." The introduction of specific, measurable goals is among the most promising yet underused strategies we can introduce into school improvement efforts.

A Symbiotic Relationship Between Goals and Teamwork

Failure to establish clear goals for schooling may explain why so much apparent collaboration is futile:

> Far too many teams casually accept goals that are neither demanding, precise, realistic, nor actually held in common.... Teamwork alone never makes a team (Katzenbach and Smith 1993, p. 21).

Goals themselves lead not only to success but also to the effectiveness and cohesion of a team. This concept is different from the conventional notion that only the "right" individuals with suitable chemistry can make an effective team or that team spirit must first be cultivated through a series of team-building activities prior to establishing goals. Viktor Frankl (1963) found that the best way to bring a group of quarrelsome boys together was to provide them with a common goal. Katzenbach and Smith (1993) made the same discovery among the dozens of teams they studied. A clear "common purpose and set of related performance goals," not personality or predisposition, promotes effective teamwork (p. 44).

Little's (1990) research corroborates this same principle: The most effective forms of collegiality succeed "quite apart from their personal friendships or dispositions," and instead depend upon "shared responsibility" for a task that individuals acting alone cannot complete (pp. 519–520). Effective collegiality is a function of having a clear task-orientation, which creates "peer pressure to live up to agreements made." Little (1987) provides an example of a team of teachers who meet with "the explicit aims of improving students' academic achievement" (pp. 494–495). We must recognize the connection between the social, spiritual vitality of a team and its single-minded commitment to performance, the most palpable form of which is a common, objective goal. Peters and Waterman acknowledge this connection:

> Nothing is more enticing than the feeling of being needed, which is the magic that produces high expectations. What's more, if it's your peers who have those high expectations of you, then there's all the more incentive to perform well (Peters and Waterman, in Fullan 1991, p. 83).

Goals and the commitment that they generate are the glue that holds teams together:

> A team's purpose and specific performance goals have a symbiotic relationship; each depends on the other to stay relevant and vital. The specific performance goals help a team track progress and hold itself accountable; the broader, even nobler aspirations in a team's purpose supply both meaning and emotional energy (Katzenbach and Smith 1993, p. 55).

The combination of goals and teamwork is essential to performance. These two elements point up the convergence of economic and social, rational, and emotional factors in improvement initiatives.

20   As Lortie (1975) and Little (1990) observed, this kind of goal-oriented teamwork is rare in schools. Rosenholtz (1991) made a related observation: The existence of common goals in schools was just as rare, and the lack of agreed-upon goals makes schools unique among organizations. She found that there was very little goal consensus—a collective agreement about what to work toward—even though her studies revealed that this element was the heart of what accounted for progress and success.

Rosenholtz (1991) also found a reciprocal relationship between goals and collegiality: Isolation "undermines the development of shared instructional goals" (p. 17). Without clear, common goals, teachers are not able to communicate meaningfully and precisely about how to improve—and about how to determine if they are improving. Clear goals "promote rational planning and action," as well as "clear criteria by which...performance can be evaluated" (p. 13). When clear goals are absent, schools become "nothing more than collections of independent teachers, each marching to the step of a different pedagogical drum" (p. 17).

At Dodge Park Elementary School in Prince George's County, Maryland, the student body was more than 90 percent poor and minority. Achievement was low—at the 44th percentile on the California Achievement Test. The school established an explicit goal: to raise poor and minority achievement. Educators worked together to develop more effective strategies and to raise expectations. Over the next four years, overall achievement went from the 44th to the 99th percentile. Minority students surpassed their white counterparts by 11 points. They outperformed other minority students in the county by 28 points (Murphy 1988).

School success depends upon how effectively we select, define, and measure progress and how well we adjust effort toward goals. School goals tell teachers what should be emphasized instructionally and define for schools and teachers "how they should gauge their performance success" (Rosenholtz 1991, p. 5).

The lack of common goals actually *promotes* isolation from colleagues, which animates a spiral of fear and insecurity as teachers perceive that their problems are unique (Rosenholtz 1989). This idea parallels Lortie's findings that teachers working in isolation are stymied in their desire to seek help from each other. These conditions interact, intensifying each other: Isolation thwarts common direction, which in turn promotes a deeper sense of isolation as teachers grow further and further apart in what they think and do and in how they pursue tacit or expressed goals. Teachers reach a point where they become set in their ways and therefore more reluctant to consider pursuing common improvement goals.

This is the world of schools. They typically lack clear, common direction and communication that promotes people working toward mutually intelligible goals.

But even goals are not enough: Goal-orientation plus dialogue brings teams closer to their goals. Such dialogue helps teams identify and address instructional and classroom factors that have the best chance of making a difference. A middle school in Richmond County, Georgia, had instituted measures to help at-risk students: lower class size, special programs, and counseling. Nothing happened. It was not until teachers began to meet in study groups to help each other implement more effective teaching strategies that results came. In one year, the average student went from making 6 month's progress to making 10 month's progress. The promotion rate increased from 30 to 70 percent. The following year, it increased again—to 95 percent (Joyce, Wolf, and Calhoun 1993).

If we wish to have energized employees who are steadily progressing toward the ultimate, long-term goal of providing a better, richer education for our students, then every member of every school should be working together in teams, not token or merely social teams, but goal-oriented units. These units are where subgoals are developed. Subgoals help students see smaller, short-term successes, which encourage long-term improvement. Figure 2.1 shows examples of subgoals.

FIGURE 2.1
Goals and Subgoals

Goal: Students will write well.
    Subgoals
- Write effective introductions.
- Provide supporting details.

Goal: Students will excel in math.
    Subgoals
- Describe and understand the steps to solve problems.
- Compute more accurately.
- Apply mathematical knowledge to practical situations.

Goal: Students will excel in science.
    Subgoals
- Demonstrate mastery of scientific knowledge.
- Conduct a rigorous experiment.
- Make a presentation proposing a solution to a scientific or technological problem.

A Goal-Averse Culture

Initially, the middle school in Richmond County, Georgia, illustrated one problem in education: Efforts are often too far removed from what should be education's primary goal—classroom results. This tendency runs deep. In reviewing 20 student action research project proposals, as well as a popular book on action research, I found only one project that expressed an interest in gauging the project's impact *on students;* the rest focused on general observation and qualitative study of teacher behaviors (which are also important). What is interesting is that in all this research, I found an apparent aversion to gauging what may be the most significant and helpful data and progress—that which reflects the goal of student learning. Our aversion to such goals is manifest.

Donahoe (1993) thinks that the free-lance culture of schools is the primary impediment. After working with a host of schools, he concluded that "schools had no organization." He once told an audience that schools were only "convenient locations for a bunch of individual teachers, like independent contractors." The audience not only accepted this rather stark assessment but "agreed rather enthusiastically" with it. Without deliberate intervention, the culture—in this case, the isolated, relatively goal-free ethos of public schools—will almost always prevail (p. 299).

John Goodlad (Goodlad et al. 1970) made the same discovery: A school's culture was one where, despite the school's intention to implement reforms or new curriculum, the conservative tendency almost always won out. The culture of isolation and privacy generally ensured that innovations were not really implemented. Despite a school's official adoption of new programs, the reality behind the classroom door was not innovative. Evidence indicated that only the most partial, superficial implementation was occurring as teachers found ways to twist the innovation right back into what they had always done.

From General to Common, Measurable Goals

Language can mislead. Efforts that are described using words such as "innovation," "goals," or "purpose" can convince us that we are engaged in substantive change when we may not be. Years into what most schools considered to be profound change, Goodlad and his associates saw no substantive evidence of that change.

Even when schools establish goals, the goals tend to be too general. This unfortunate case of "general goals" creates a sense of "false clarity"—the erroneous belief that we understand and know how to work toward achieving the goals (Fullan 1991, pp. 34–35). Conversely, common, specific goals require teamwork to develop common approaches to reaching the goals (Katzenbach and Smith 1993). Such activity promotes clarity and intelligibility and facilitates team members' ability to learn from each other's experience.

I believe that specific goals are the most vital ingredient of purpose. Improvement cannot occur without them. It is no coincidence that Deming's first principle is, "Create constancy of purpose" (1986, p. 23). And a look at Mary Walton's books (1986, 1990) on the success of Deming's methods reveals how closely connected this purpose is to specific, unambiguous goals—reducing turnaround time and waste, meeting deadlines, and meeting or exceeding quality standards.

Why is this specificity so crucial? Rosenholtz (1989) found a number of reasons:

- Specific goals convey a message directly to teachers that they are capable of improvement.
- Specific goals provide a basis for rational decision making, for ways to organize and execute their instruction.
- Specific goals enable teachers to gauge their success.
- Specific goals promote professional dialogue.

Clear goals require us to provide feedback about our progress toward them. This feedback, the vital, frequent flow of information, ensures against the "twisting" Goodlad describes. One cannot twist an innovation when teachers share and examine the feedback about the processes that produce results. Such regular feedback is the key to successful implementation:

> Specific performance goals are an integral part of purpose. Transforming broad directives into specific and measurable performance goals is the surest first step for a team trying to shape a common purpose (Katzenbach and Smith 1993, p. 53).

And yet, institutionally, we continue to ignore the need for feedback. We cherish our typically private, imprecise preferences at the expense of clear and collective goal-orientation. We thus forfeit progress.

Goal-Orientation at Centennial Elementary School

Collective, efficacious, accelerated improvement must of necessity be somewhat public, with the potential for reward—and a measure of risk—which this publicity implies. Centennial Elementary School in Evans, Colorado (Andrade and Ryley 1992), shows how

24

teachers resolved this tension. They have been known to exchange high fives at meetings when they reach monthly improvement goals. But they had to wade through the initial discomfort of allowing the entire school see how each grade level performed relative to the schoolwide goal of improving student writing skills.

Reflective of the school's TQM approach, student performance results are collected, charted, and analyzed at regular monthly meetings. Teachers see student progress, both at grade level and school level, on a 7-point rubric used throughout the district. To reduce risk (of killing the project), teams report *anonymously*; individual teacher accomplishments are not revealed. But each grade-level team does know that as a member of that school they are expected to perform at a high level. This regular, focused interaction, working toward a common goal, ensures that Centennial teachers speak the same language—the key, as we have seen, to teachers being able to help each other.

The result? Prior to instituting the new process, the schools' writing scores were 16th in a 16-school district for two years. The year they began this goal-oriented approach, they went from 16th to 4th. The power of these simple principles cannot be underestimated.

In contrast to such clear goal-orientation, Carl Glickman's (1993) experience is worth pondering. It reveals the great distance that still separates us from the many ways of establishing specific, measurable goals for schools. Glickman found himself addressing the faculty of an award-winning school. He asked them to name their school's objectives. The faculty's enthusiastic response was, "To integrate technology into the curriculum."

He thought they misunderstood him. He rephrased it. "No," he said, "What I mean is, what are you trying to accomplish for students?"

The principal then responded, with enthusiastic nods from teachers, that their goal was, "To show that our school can move into the 21st century through technology" (p. 48).

Glickman, with a "nagging feeling of disbelief," stopped pressing them. But during the next few weeks, he asked the same question at 20 other schools. Their responses were telling. Here are examples of the goals they had set:

- Implement whole-language instruction in every classroom.
- Use cooperative learning.
- Develop portfolios and performance assessments.
- Assess learning styles.

Glickman, who has helped many schools improve, believes that such goals are "typical of most 'with it' schools." When he asked people at such schools how they would determine progress and achievement, their responses "reaffirmed his gnawing unrest." They replied that they would gauge their success on whether the innovation had been implemented—*rather than by whether students had learned* (1993, p. 49).

The history of education reveals numerous attempts to ensure that all teachers have learned to use certain innovations. What is less certain is the depth of that learning, whether learning was even remotely connected to student growth—the ostensible intent of education and efforts to improve it.

What should goals look like? Glickman differentiates between innovations, which he criticizes, and what he calls objectives (another word for goals) (see Figure 2.2). What is the difference? Objectives can be assessed, and success toward them can be measured. Glickman believes that the "litmus test for a good school is not its innovations but rather the solid, purposeful, enduring *results* it tries to obtain for its students" (1993, p. 50) (emphasis added).

FIGURE 2.2
Innovations Compared to Objectives

Innovation	Objective
Technology	Students will learn how to use various forms of technology to improve their performance.
Cooperative Learning	Students will learn how to operate in groups, and their achievement and attitudes will reflect the skills learned.
Whole-Language Instruction	Students will acquire a more positive attitude toward reading, read with more comprehension, and write more creatively and analytically.
Interdisciplinary Instruction	Students will be better able to solve problems by drawing from the various disciplines.

Goals: The Missing Piece in Reform

When specific goals do not exist, one-shot staff development or high-sounding programs often fill the void. Reporting that an entire staff learned a new program or method is easy; easier still is presuming that this new practice or program will benefit students. But the

26   evidence is clear: Most of what goes on in the name of innovation has a limited impact on student learning.

School reform or restructuring—for example, site-based management—has had disappointing results (Malen, Ogawa, and Kranz 1990). We must remind ourselves that like all innovations, such reforms initially arrived carrying the promise of better results. Site-based management's primary selling point was that it would wrest control from tired, self-serving bureaucracies and turn it over to people whose interests would ensure that schools and school systems would produce better student learning results.

What happened? Not much, according to several studies:

- Despite the time and resources devoted to this huge, widely adopted effort, no documented effect on student learning as a result of site-based management exists (Fullan 1993).
- In Kentucky, where site-based councils have been in place for several years, the councils were no better than the old bureaucracies at focusing on learning. Even an advocate for the changes there admits that site councils have yet to understand that the "ultimate purpose of the councils is to advance student learning" (David 1994, p. 711).
- The outgoing superintendent of Dade County schools, a mecca for those wanting to institute site-based management, left there saying that the impact on achievement "was a wash."
- In Chicago, where the much-heralded move to site-based management seemed so full of promise, the result was no result—not on student learning or even on "the teaching-learning process" (Fullan 1993, p. 123).

We are now in the middle of another major reform: Many schools and districts have adopted some form of TQM initiative. Will it go the way of site-based management (with which it is frequently confused)? The signs are not good. Examples of real success, even in districts where the effort is well under way, are rare. A recent review of almost 100 articles reveals the same disturbing tendency to avoid a concern with goals, with striving for measurable results. Only five articles featured an explicit reference to concrete goals or results, either already achieved or anticipated. Only two goals were related to student learning; one was to improve student scores on weekly spelling tests, an innocuous but hardly inspiring focus. The remaining goals dealt with processes and activities, elaborate planning, partnerships, and new arrangements.

If we concentrate our efforts more on measurable goals, then site-based management and Total Quality Management will thrive. I do not mean that all school goals must be academic learning goals. Salient goals for processes and products are needed, too. But the last 10 years should have taught us that establishing vague process or procedural goals in the absence of clear, concrete learning goals is foolish. Each undergirds the other. Learning goals give meaning to and act as a healthy check on the traditionally untethered tendency for public institutions to be satisfied with processes, regardless of outcomes.

Osborne and Gaebler (1992), the authors of *Reinventing Government: How the Entrepreneurial Spirit Is Transforming the Public Sector,* do not believe that schools have a good record of maintaining a strong or sufficient sense of purpose. They think that without the profit motive, schools do not have enough incentive to establish and pursue palpable improvement. Our record of pouring huge amounts of time and resources into processes (e.g., site-based management), without establishing improved student learning as the goal, probably shocks anyone outside the education establishment.

If we had connected learning goals to site-based management 10 years ago, we would no doubt have much to celebrate now. Because we did not, we have added to a legacy of disillusionment. And we have consumed untold amounts of what Glickman says is the "scarcest resource in school renewal"—time (1993, p. 44).

Conditions That Encourage Goals

If we want goals to proliferate, we need to create a climate hospitable to them and to the hard-working individuals who can help us reach them. Peter Senge (1990) is right: If we want better results, we need to look beyond the isolated point or moment or result and into the system that affects the impact we can have. And right now, that system is insensitive to the fact that people work best in a climate that creates high expectations but mitigates against personal threat. Even Susan Rosenholtz (1991), for whom goals is a mantra, found again and again that people's willingness to learn from each other and to work hard and persistently toward a challenging goal was a function of a workplace that is not "ego-endangering." Rick Stiggins's work shows that using explicit goals may make teachers more vulnerable to criticism:

> To the extent that you are clear and specific about the outcomes that you take on as your instructional responsibility, you open yourself up to the possibility that some of your students may not be able to hit the target after instruction and there will exist concrete, irrefutable assessment evidence of

28

this....In effect, your supervisor may be able to...muster evidence that you did not succeed in doing what you were hired to do—produce achievement results (1994, p. 64).

Without abandoning the importance of high expectations, sustained change must rely on the human factors that account for a sense of satisfaction, of what Deming repeatedly calls "joy in labor" throughout his work and presentations. Kevin Castner, former assistant superintendent of schools in Frederick County, Maryland, calls it "organized enthusiasm." As we have seen, goals are the key. They tap into a basic sense of accomplishment and improvement that makes life interesting and challenging.

We know more now that we did 26 years ago, when Goodlad noted the absence of clear, specific learning goals at every level of our school systems. We recognize how crucial goals are to improvement. It is time we got around to making such goals a universal expectation at every level and school.

3

Performance Data

When people say they work at a good school, what do they mean?

—Glickman 1993

But what does "pretty well" mean? chided Ralph.

—Byham 1992

What gets measured gets done.

—Peters 1987

Data help monitor and assess performance. Just as goals are an essential element of success, so data are an essential piece of working toward goals. As with goals, data must be used judiciously and with discretion.

Lortie writes that "the monitoring of effective instruction is the heart of effective instruction" (1975, p. 141). Colorado's Weld County School District 6 applied this concept when teachers decided to systematically raise overall achievement while addressing the obvious disparities between socioeconomic groups. They introduced many interventions, including a system in which students had to demonstrate competency in writing, reading, and mathematics before graduating to the next level. Students had to move up before moving on.

A crucial component of their new effort was collecting data both monthly and quarterly. The system enables students to know how they are performing, which helps them focus on continually improving. The system also helps teachers:

> [Teachers] can base teaching decisions on solid data rather than on assumptions, and they can make adjustments early on to avoid the downward spiral of remediation (Waters, Burger, and Burger 1995, p. 39).

29

30   Does such a system, as some suspect, result in pushing low-achievers down even further? Hardly. Overall achievement has increased, and the gap between rich and poor has closed considerably—even in such higher-order competencies as writing. Figure 3.1 shows what happened in District 6 after educators introduced a writing assessment during the 1988–89 school year.

FIGURE 3.1

Writing Assessment Results for Weld County School District 6 in Colorado

Gap Reduction Among Socioeconomic (SES) Groups

Source: Waters, Burger, and Burger 1995, p. 37.

Data are to goals what signposts are to travelers; data are not end points, but data are essential to reaching them—the signposts on the road to school improvement. Thus, data and feedback are interchangeable. Although schools rarely use data and results to inform practice (Rosenholtz 1991), data should be an essential feature of how schools do business.

The Call for Data

Practitioners frequently say that data do not belong in the educational sphere. Alfie Kohn (1993), in a critique of the TQM movement in schools, expresses a concern with data. He is afraid that emphasizing the measurable will force a shift toward areas that are most easily measured (e.g., spelling tests), or that we will begin to rely on standardized tests and exclude all other measures. Point taken. But we have already seen how teachers are using data to track and improve achievement in writing and higher-order math skills (see Chapter 1). We see other examples in Chapters 6 and 7. Criteria-based assessments and rubrics have changed the nature of assessment by providing numerical data that take us beyond the ability to test mere recall. We can now assess understanding, application, and other thinking skills in new ways.

It is one thing to be circumspect to protect against the abuses or excesses of data; it is something else to flatly reject their use. Are gathering and analyzing data on progress and achievement not needed? Umpteen reforms have come and gone, using up time, money, optimism, and hope. They have left a crippling disillusion-ment in their wake, a cynicism about staff development and any belief that training or innovation benefits students. Not using data to monitor results can be calamitous. Recent examples are those foundations that after spending billions of dollars in grants to inno-vate, made an interesting discovery: No salient attempt had been made to measure the effects of the innovations (West 1994). Carnine (1993) writes that our current practices for adopting classroom ma-terials and programs, because they do not use achievement data, are at odds with "the results educators and the public are clamoring for" (p. 40). These materials are never classroom tested. He laments the irony of this in light of the 309 billion hours U.S. students spend in schools using such materials.

How long will we continue to avoid using an invaluable tool, capable of telling us how we are doing, what is and is not working, and how to adjust effort toward improvement? Most educators know that we do not adequately monitor student progress. If we did, Grant Wiggins's remark (which I heard him make at a conference in Phoenix, Ariz.) would not invariably get a reaction from audiences:

> Schools don't pilot anything. They just send ideas and inno-vations off and wave at them from the pier, never to be seen again.

Share this quote with a group of educators; the eruption of knowing laughter says it all. If we look at Deming's "Plan, Do, Study, Act" cycle (1986) (or any of its educational equivalents in the James Comer or Henry Levin schools), we can see that we do, do, do, but seldom study. We fail to examine data that can guide us as we act. No wonder implementation is so often haphazard and why so many innovations do not have the expected impact.

32   Many enlightened educators recognize that we need data to improve teaching practice:

- In the early 1980s, Ron Edmonds advocated for a more rigorous and frequent concern with performance data when he wrote that "the days are long gone when an educator's best judgement constitutes sufficient proof of learning outcomes." One of the principles of effective schools that he fathered is that successful schools "frequently monitor progress" (Edmonds, in Bullard and Taylor 1993, p. 17).
- For Grant Wiggins, a serious problem facing education is "the failure of classroom teachers...to be results focused and data driven. Coaches regularly adjust performance in light of ongoing results" (1994a, p. 18).
- Matthew Miles tells us that "those steering school improvement need good data on what is happening" (Miles, in Fullan 1991, p. 83).
- Jacqueline and Martin Brooks (1993), in their excellent book about active, constructivist teaching, write that "school-based study groups" must begin "systematically collecting, analyzing, and using these data to inform classroom practices" (p. 125).
- Bruce Joyce and his colleagues (1993), in the name of action research, exhort us to "collect, organize, and interpret on-site data" (p. 8).
- Carl Glickman (1993) urges us to ask for "clear indicators: What data or information about effectiveness are currently collected? How complete are the data?... How does the school community share the data and use them for setting priorities and determining actions?" (p. 51).
- Henry Levin and his associates (Hopfenberg, Levin, Meister, and Roers 1990) call for school improvement that uses "data, on students...qualitative and quantitative information...disaggregated test scores and other measures of student performance" (p. 14).
- Principal Suzanne Still led her faculty in creating a remarkable turnaround at an accelerated school, Hollibrook Elementary, outside Houston. She believed that action and accomplishments must be seen in "concrete terms....All staff need to become data collectors" (Still, in Schmoker and Wilson 1993, p. 86).

Michael Fullan (1991) not only emphasizes the importance of data to evaluate and monitor progress and monitor results, he also stresses the role of data gathering:

> Gathering data...is also crucial. The success of implementation
> is highly dependent on the establishment of effective ways of
> getting information on how well or poorly change is going in
> the school or classroom (p. 87).

Stressing the connection between teamwork and collectively analyzing data, Fullan adds that "the crux of the matter is getting the right people together with the right information at their disposal" (1991, p. 87). Goals are implicit in this scheme. But local information and data that inform our collaborative effort to reach our goals are essential.

Part of the reason we dismiss this call for data is the outworn mind-set that because schools are so different from other organizations, quality and learning will thrive spontaneously, without any formal effort to use data equivalent to what other organizations use routinely. Schools generally avoid goals and precise means of measuring progress toward them.

We typically hesitate to use data as signposts to assess where we are and where we are headed. Rosenholtz (1991) found that "despite schools' espoused goals of student learning, principals rarely use data on student achievement to evaluate teachers or to monitor student performance even though such data are frequently available" (p. 16).

Fear of Data and Results

Even though goals positively influence improvement, few schools "measure progress against both the ideal outcome and the actual baseline." Such data promote conflict, revealing inconsistencies among teachers and between intent and actual results (Evans 1993, p. 23).

Why do we avoid data? The reason is fear—of data's capacity to reveal strength and weakness, failure and success. Education seems to maintain a tacit bargain among constituents at every level not to gather or use information that will reveal where we need to do better, where we need to make changes. Data almost always point to action—they are the enemy of comfortable routines. By ignoring data, we promote inaction and inefficiency.

Just as Stiggins (1994) saw how fear of retribution may suppress using explicit goals (see Chapter 2), so, too, can performance data generate fear. This fear helps explain the apparent contradiction between the obvious pleasure that educators would take in improved "achievement results" (Stiggins 1994, p. 64) and their wariness about setting goals that are a necessary precondition for the results.

Fatalism feeds fear. Teachers have a limited confidence in their ability to "raise achievement." A few years in the system typically undermines whatever confidence they may have had about their ability to significantly affect groups of children (Lortie 1975, p. 127). This undermining begins even before teachers arrive at school; their professional training does not include closely examining and discuss-

34   ing successful schools or models. Without this training, new teachers arrive tacitly accepting that schools are generally "stuck" institutions, where the only triumphs are personal or infrequent (Lortie 1975, p. 121).

In such a climate, any expectation for improvement seems unrealistic—and generates fear. Teachers regard specific goals as a threat: Will I, can we actually make an impact—a measurable impact? This doubt combines with the fear that failure to reach goals will be used against them. Feedback will be used as evidence that they are failures. "Monitoring results…is frequently misused.…In the early attempts at change, people are usually wary of gathering information" (performance data) (Fullan 1991, p. 87). This fear can be seen at every level—from district, to school, to individual classroom teachers. In the classroom, consider the absurdity of the ritual evaluation that teachers undergo; it has virtually no connection to what a teacher has or has not accomplished as an individual or a team member. Such a process helps make the "evaluation boondoggle," as Glickman tells us, "perhaps the greatest robbery of educational resources in our time" (1991, p. 7).

This fear of results, of accountability, influenced the impact of outcome-based education (OBE). A majority of schools that set out to respond to the cry to become more outcome based did not act, finding numerous ways to postpone becoming results oriented, which was a major part of what "outcome-based" was supposed to mean. Having ever so gingerly put our toes into the cold waters of change, we realized that change would require something like accountability, which we have never warmed toward. We stepped back and took refuge in the much easier and more traditional activity of defining and redefining outcomes—a safer pursuit that has postponed improvement.

Reducing Threat from Setting Goals and Using Data

My discussion is not intended to blame anyone; instead, it is aimed at understanding a system that avoids using precise information that can guide and inform better teaching practice. Goal-setting that uses data to monitor progress can be a threatening endeavor. Preparation and ongoing training have often failed to provide teachers with the ability or confidence to believe they can succeed. This insecurity hampers every teacher and administrator, including our most talented and industrious.

We can reduce this threat without eliminating accountability by following some guidelines:

• **Do not use data primarily to identify or eliminate poor teachers.** Such action sends fear throughout the organization and thus encourages avoidance, sabotage, and fudging of data. The usefulness of data is worth more to the best 95 percent of our teachers than to the least effective 5 percent.

• **Do not introduce high stakes prematurely.** Part of the reason that schools in Littleton, Colorado, failed in their attempt to institute OBE was the revelation that only 6 percent of the students could succeed in the new higher-order math performance. Because the assessment had been made a requirement for graduation, parents and students were afraid they would not graduate. Furor replaced reasoned negotiation (Association for Supervision and Curriculum Development 1994).

• **Try to collect and analyze data collaboratively and anonymously by team, department, grade level, or school.** Ensure to the greatest possible extent that those closest to the point of implementation, the practitioners, analyze the data. When possible, let the team exercise its own accountability.

• **Be cautious in implementing pay-for-performance schemes, especially in the beginning.** When data are used for evaluation, institute a "true 'appeal' system," which allows schools or teams to "reject, if necessary, targets handed down to them" (Peters 1987, p. 512). Teachers work under difficult conditions, making only a modest amount of collaboration and reflection possible. Peters believes the emphasis should be on measurable progress toward reachable, conservative goals.

• **Allow teachers, by school or team, as much autonomy as possible in selecting the kind of data they think will be most helpful.** The data must accurately reflect teacher *and* student performance and be properly aligned with state, district, and school goals and expectations. Establish clear criteria that promote a relevant, substantive focus.

• **Inundate practitioners with success stories that include data.** The stories should stress how measurable success is attainable when we select the right goals—manageable ones—and employ the most effective and proven strategies for reaching them.

These measures not only eliminate fear but also promote team spirit and the uninhibited, continuous knowledge-sharing that are the chief benefits of collective effort. Wrongly used, data have a chilling effect. But data can become a force for improvement by energizing those closest to their work. Most of all, data promote the flow of pertinent information and emerging expertise that is the

36   lifeblood of optimism and improvement. Even though teachers are
           initially wary of gathering data, something quite different takes over
           when the right kind of improvement process is under way:

> Teachers and others close to implementation are those most
> insistent on gathering and examining the results of their
> efforts. Good change processes develop trust and the desire to
> get better results (Fullan 1991, p. 87).

Despite the tendency to avoid or mistrust those calling for results,
teachers will find that data and results can be a powerful force for
generating an intrinsic desire to improve. Properly done, "accountability and improvement can be effectively interwoven, but it requires great sophistication" (Fullan 1991, p. 87). Such effort means
making accountability more friendly and nonthreatening. A concern
with results and improvement can satisfy and energize every con-
stituent, from the practitioner, to the parent, to the school board.

When results and improvement energize people, they want to
see progress toward meaningful goals. Csikszentmihalyi tells about a
factory worker whose goal is to complete his assembly-line duties
with ever-greater speed and efficiency—one second at a time. For him
work is "more fun than watching television" (1990, p. 159). Centennial Elementary School teachers also demonstrate the energizing
effect of reaching goals using data:

> Cheers go up as groups plot improvement on the graphs and
> charts posted around the room. Colleagues share high fives
> because they have not only reached goals, but have exceeded
> them. Staff members share an enthusiasm and focus that
> simply did not exist in the school before (Andrade and Ryley
> 1992, p. 22).

Goal-orientation. Focus. Enthusiasm. Is this work or play? At one
of our schools, Mesa Verde Elementary, measurable gains during the
school year resulted in high levels of enthusiasm and desire for more
improvement. After seeing the data at an evening meeting, one
teacher called another at home; the news could not wait until the
next morning. Performance data and feedback—forms of results—
nourish that sense of forward movement that is the enemy of
boredom. We must establish the right conditions for data to be
regarded as useful tools, overcoming that initial wariness and building trust.

Group Data Versus Conventional Data

Collective pride and enthusiasm are the result of an organized
effort to monitor and adjust progress based on data. Interestingly,

one of the first things we hear when the subject of data is brought up is, "We already collect data. We always have." To be sure, teachers do have data, such as Individual Education Plans (IEPs), grades, grade-point averages, and test scores. Though such individual data are useful, they are seldom converted into the kind of group data that is necessary for more formal and collective reflection and analysis. Even such easily gathered, conventional data are seldom collectively analyzed to help teams or schools find better ways to address collective problems. They could be.

Teachers tend to evaluate students individually and reflect on how to improve class performance less frequently. "We would expect," writes Lortie (1975), "to find heavy emphasis on results attained with classes," as opposed to results with individual students. But only 29 percent of those teachers whom he studied "mentioned generalized outcomes with entire classes" as a source of pride (p. 127). Evaluating individual students is analogous to a grounds keeper managing one section of a lawn. Lortie found that educators do not seek to identify and address patterns of success and failure, which can have broad and continuous benefits for greater numbers of children. Not focusing on patterns is unfortunate, because the real power of data emerges when they enable us to see patterns of instructional program strengths or weaknesses, thus multiplying the number of individual students we can help.

Lortie (1975) discovered that despite the absence of concern with group outcomes, most teachers did embrace the ideal of "reaching *all* students" (p. 131). But a stark disparity between this ideal and an acceptance of something less than the ideal was apparent. Teachers usually spoke about success in terms of having reached a single student or small group and did not presume that they could have a more general influence. Has teacher training, which emphasizes the individual child, left teachers "unprepared to think about measurements for *groups* of children?" (p. 128).

We are passing up one of education's greatest unexploited opportunities. If leadership provided the encouragement and opportunity for practitioners to begin gathering and examining collective student results, we would make real strides toward understanding our strengths and weaknesses. An examination of collective or aggregate analysis (e.g., the number of students at or above standard) not only promotes a common goal-orientation but also brings forth the insights of many minds. Such analysis breaks down the cellular structure of schools and furnishes a precious perspective that can only be heard in communion with others whose struggles are similar. Group data maximize our ability to develop the most effective improvement and corrective action and to focus that action on the highest-priority areas, those with the greatest opportunity for improvement. If we

38   want many students to benefit from our efforts, we must work to solve the problems that they face. Such patterns and priorities do not emerge spontaneously; rather, they require formal, though not time-consuming, collection and analysis. Some teams in our district are making steady progress toward goals by meeting monthly or quarterly for only about 30 minutes (see Appendix). A team leader at one elementary school pointed out that she can gather and chart the data in about 15 minutes. Then the team can discuss what is and is not working and how to get better results the next time.

Data: Making the Invisible Visible

You cannot fight what you cannot see. A group of teachers at one of our schools could not see that student difficulty in demonstrating mathematical processes in writing was a problem of the greatest magnitude until the teachers gathered data using a math rubric they had developed. Very little discussion was necessary at that point. Five minutes of brainstorming generated 10 concrete improvement strategies, three of which became their focus for the next month. The next month's results? Twenty percent more students could reach proficiency in this skill. Data enable us to make efficient use of even short opportunities for collaboration.

Data make the invisible visible, revealing strengths and weaknesses that are easily concealed. Data promote certainty and precision, which increases teachers' confidence in their abilities. In their studies, both Lortie and Rosenholtz observed a high degree of "teacher uncertainty" (Lortie 1975, p. 132; Rosenholtz 1991, p. 69). Clear goals and ways to assess progress toward them were highly effective in reducing this uncertainty (Rosenholtz 1991). Most schools are too poorly organized to see the connection between effort and accomplishment.

In many organizations, the employees' vague sense that they are not having a meaningful impact can impede progress (Senge 1990). "Tangibility" is the word Lortie (1975) uses to describe a concrete sense that one is making a difference (p. 126). He illustrates its meaning by contrasting an athletic coach's sense of accomplishment with a win-loss record (tangibility) to teachers' vague sense that their efforts benefit students. Performance data gathered and analyzed by a team, group, or faculty not only break down isolation and promote meaningful sharing, they also reveal the impact teachers are having—or not having. Such activity feeds goal-oriented effort as well as personal pride and satisfaction. Data and feedback, forms of results, are the primary ingredients for promoting sustained effort toward goals:

We assert...that goal-setting activities accentuate those instructional objectives toward which teachers should aim their
improvement efforts; that principals, through their frequent
monitoring of teachers' progress, specify improvement needs
and mobilize school resources (Rosenholtz 1991, pp. 6–7).

Rosenholtz found both to be rare in the 78 schools she studied.

Once goals are established, teachers can monitor progress, and
goals and data can begin to exert a positive influence. Combined with
collaboration, goals and data create conditions that "enable if not
compel individual teachers to request and offer advice in helping
their colleagues" (Rosenholtz 1991, p. 6). This conformity constrains
absolute autonomy, which Rosenholtz found prevalent in the least-
effective schools. As Peters and Waterman (1982) have pointed out,
conforming to communal norms not only promotes productivity but
can be positive and pleasurable.

Common goals that are regularly evaluated against common
measures—data—sustain collective focus and reveal the best opportunities for practitioners to learn from each other and hence to get
better results. At Mesa Verde Elementary School, data on writing
improvement revealed students' pace and progress, which enabled
teachers to begin focused, productive dialogue. During the first year
that improvements were instituted, the number of students writing
at or above grade level rose from 12 percent in August to 32 percent
in November, schoolwide. Between November and January, scores
rose again, to 41 percent; between January and March, to 51 percent.
By May, 73 percent of the students were writing at or above grade
level. The school's goal is to increase that percentage next year. At
one meeting I attended, teachers generated numerous concrete ideas
to promote success and address difficulties. Several are included here:

- Model the writing process by having the entire class compose
an essay and write it on the board.
- Ask students who are strong in one area to help others who
are having trouble in that area.
- Help students brainstorm lists of topics that interest them so
that they can draw from the lists when asked to write.

Revealing Where Improvement Is Needed

We must take advantage of data's capacity to prompt collaborative dialogue. Deming saw, like few others, that measurement had
power for revealing opportunities for improvement and hence for
generating ideas and releasing energy in the service of quality. Data
allow the essential points of "leverage" (Senge 1990, p. 114) to

40   emerge, where concealed challenges and opportunities are put in vivid relief:

- John Goodlad's famous study (1984) showed that more than 90 percent of what students do in a normal day consists of boring, passive activities (Fiske 1992).
- Only 11 percent of school districts nationwide disaggregate data to ensure that they can see and thus address the needs of their lowest-achieving populations (Bullard and Taylor 1993).
- According to one study, 90 percent of teachers had never visited another teacher's classroom to observe them and then to "discuss what they could learn from each other" (Glickman 1991, p. 7).
- Second grade teachers at Donaldson Elementary School in our district reviewed stories that 2nd graders had written and discovered that only about 5 of 90 students could write a satisfactory descriptive setting. Effective settings became a priority.
- National Assessment of Educational Progress data reveal that only 3 percent of students nationwide are proficient writers (Olson 1994a).

Objections

Data can convey the magnitude of a problem; they can arrest our attention, establish our priorities, and reveal progress that motivates and sustains us in our efforts. Nonetheless, there are objections to their use.

Schools are not automobile plants; schools cannot control the variables that affect data and outcomes. Many feel that data speak of hard facts in a seemingly "soft" world—that of schools. An automobile plant and a school have significant distinctions: Students are not raw material that we can select or discard; learning is a far less rigid—and therefore less measurable—commodity than automobiles.

This type of thinking may reflect the old fatalism, which prevails in a system that so infrequently provides what the most successful schools, programs, and practices can offer. We sell ourselves short. We *can* influence variables that affect outcomes. The educational system, which includes preservice training, staff development, and teacher induction, needs to disseminate and study success both within and beyond our own schools and districts. We need to learn from those few successful schools and teachers who have acted on practices that have the highest probability for improved results. For example, one of our high school teachers implemented a sound, research-based approach to reading instruction to improve the performance of her 33 Chapter I students (Carbo 1986). In four months (one semester), the results were impressive:

- One student's reading level improved 4.1 years.
- Six students gained between 3 and 4 years.
- Eight students gained between 2 and 3 years.
- Ten students gained between 1 and 2 years.

Similarly, the Success for All program has raised reading scores dramatically in many of the schools where it was implemented. Improvements typically start in the first year (Slavin, Madden, Dolan, Wasik, Ross, and Smith 1994). Such successes make talk about deficient raw material seem irrelevant. They certainly force us to reconsider the inevitability that is implicit in the notion that "the character of a school's output depends largely on the school's input, namely the characteristics of the entering children" (Sarason 1982, p. 268). This statement was probably true in a majority of cases when Sarason wrote it, but evidence now abounds that ordinary teachers can do extraordinary things—or at least realize incremental improvement with all kinds of "raw material."

We don't have time to be statisticians. Many presume that data come from the statistical arena, that teachers will be forced to master difficult or arcane formulas and thus add yet another time-consuming element to an already crowded schedule. Consultants and some educators inadvertently foster this notion. The reigning perception is that collecting and analyzing data are tantamount to calculating statistics, which is a highly specialized endeavor best left to experts. In reality, only an occasional need for using sophisticated statistical formulas arises. And for those times, experts should be used. But using data does not always require an expert to tell teachers if they have done well. Most data require only the ability to count and calculate percentages. Any conscientious teacher or team of teachers can do this activity.

I had lunch with an engineer who had participated in many different TQM improvement efforts in industry. I asked him how frequently employees needed to use sophisticated formulas to track progress. He said seldom—if ever. A walk through Allied Signal Corporation in Tucson, Arizona (whose stock has tripled since they instituted continuous improvement procedures), shows a pervasive interest in data. On the wall in every department is a colorful column chart or scatter diagram made with a ruler and felt markers. Most showed monthly progress relative to such simple goals as increasing the number of quality products produced or decreasing the number of defects per thousand. Gathering this data and updating the charts take minimal time.

Tom Peters calls such "back-of-the-envelope" calculations the real tools for improvement. Companies such as the successful GM-

42   Toyota NUMMI plant in California do not use "complex measurement techniques" (Peters 1987, p. 483). Cheap and simple tools, such as pencils and chalk, work fine. Interestingly, the examples of progress in Mary Walton's books (1986, 1990), detailing the success of TQM efforts, are similarly simple: a reduction in the number of days or hours needed to complete a process or deliver a product; a reduction in the amount of employee turnover; and the amount of time or money saved. Examples of such simple data and calculations can also be found in education:

• Teachers at George Westinghouse Vocational and Technical School in inner-city Brooklyn enjoyed simply calculated triumphs when they reduced the amount of class cutting by 39 percent and decreased the amount of students failing every class by 92 percent.

• Centennial Elementary School does nothing more than plot monthly the percentage of students who are writing proficiently and put the data on handmade bar graphs. Teachers at one of our middle schools, La Cima, plotted the percentage decrease in such behavioral areas as violent fights, incidents of classroom disruption, bus conduct, and unexcused absences—all immediately available on the computer. Their efforts resulted in significant decreases in six of seven areas.

These kinds of data are neither complex nor time consuming to collect and graph. As the examples demonstrate, there are many simple, time-efficient ways for any teacher or team of teachers to gather and display data.

Data can help us confront what we may wish to avoid and what is difficult to perceive, trace, or gauge; data can substantiate theories, inform decisions, impel action, marshal support, thwart misperceptions and unwarranted optimism, maintain focus and goal-orientation, and capture and sustain collective energy and momentum. Data help us answer the primary question "What do we do next?" amid the panoply of competing opportunities for action. Systems theorist Peter Senge calls the place where effort is needed most the greatest point of "leverage," because that is where effort will have the greatest benefit (1990, p. 114). To find these points of leverage, we must continue to ask challenging questions:

• What are data telling us? What problems or challenges do they reveal?

• What can we do about what data reveal? What strategies should we brainstorm? What research should we consult?

• What are data telling us about how effective our current efforts are in helping achieve our goals?

Data can be effective tools for promoting improvement. They can never be totally accurate or reliable, but in the hands of conscientious professionals, they promote successful, goal-oriented effort. We cannot afford to indulge in a sophomoric skepticism that absolves us of the responsibility to look at and act on information that tells us how well or not well we are doing.

Successes: Cause for Celebration

Collecting and analyzing data show schools how they are progressing toward improving their practice. The following successes illustrate how data create occasions to celebrate palpable progress.

At the end of the movie *Stand and Deliver,* Jaime Escalante's character is walking down a corridor of Garfield High School in east Los Angeles. He has just discovered that 18 of his students—a record number—have passed the AP Calculus exam. The year is 1982. The movie screen shows his subsequent successes:

- 1983, 30 of his students passed the exam.
- 1984, 63 passed the exam.
- 1985, 77 passed the exam.
- 1986, 78 passed the exam.
- 1987, 87 passed the exam.

These numbers vividly represent Escalante's accomplishments. They add a dimension to a bland statement like "Jaime Escalante is a good teacher." Escalante said that this information enables him to adjust and improve the following year.

At Central Park East, college attendance is an explicit priority. Students begin to discuss and make visits to prospective colleges with their teachers during their junior and senior years. Data showed that about 95 percent of the students who attend this school, which is in a predominantly poor neighborhood, attend college.

The Pomperaug Regional School District in Connecticut is proud of the steady gains students have made on performance assessments. Data from 1994–95 show how they compare with students in other Connecticut districts that are in the same socioeconomic category (educational reference group, or ERG). On performance assessments in math, writing, and reading, at every grade tested (4, 6, and 8), students were either tied with or ahead of their comparison group. Figure 3.2 shows how students in the Pomperaug Regional School District compared to those in other Connecticut school districts in reading.

At Apollo High School, an alternative program in Simi Valley, California, efforts to help alienated students led to significant progress. Before entering the program, 80 percent of the students were using drugs weekly; 80 percent were missing more than 70 percent

44

of their classes; and 30 percent were on probation. After entering the program, 70 percent of the students improved their attendance; the percentage of students using drugs dropped by 60 percent, and only 5 percent were on probation. Eighty-six percent graduated from high school—a remarkable achievement for an alternative program (Greene and Uroff 1989).

FIGURE 3.2
Percentage of Students Who Attained Performance Assessment Standard in Reading at Connecticut Schools in the Same Socioeconomic Category

| | PERCENT | |
Grade	Pomperaug Regional School District	Other School Districts
4	64	53
6	73	70
8	79	71

Source: K. Michael Hibbard, assistant superintendent, Pomperaug Regional School District 15, Connecticut.

The state of Maryland introduced an initiative to promote better writing skills for all students. In a 10-year period, the percentage of students meeting the state standard rose steadily each year—from 47 percent in 1984 to 92 percent in 1994.

Nancie Atwell was a teacher in a small, rural school in Boothbay Harbor, Maine. She worked hard to teach her students to become skilled, versatile writers. In 1985, her 8th graders took Maine's state writing exam. The results are shown below (Atwell 1987):

- 20 percent of her students scored at the 99th percentile.
- Almost half the students scored above the 90th percentile.
- The mean score was at the 87th percentile.

The Johnson City School District in New York State has a national reputation for being focused and data driven. In 1972, 45 to 50 percent of the students were achieving at or above grade level. Six years later, using their outcomes-driven model, the district increased the percent to 70.

Fort Pitt Elementary School is located in urban Pittsburgh. In 1993, only 1 percent of 4th graders and 3 percent of 5th graders scored at or above the national norm in writing on the Metropolitan

Achievement Test. One year later, after the school introduced an inquiry-based approach to research projects, 30 percent of 4th graders and 50 percent of 5th graders scored at or above the norm (Hartmann, DeCicco, and Griffin 1994).

A school improvement consortium called the North Carolina Project set out to make science more engaging by introducing a hands-on curriculum. In one year, the percent of students expressing their enthusiasm for science rose from 38 to 87 percent (O'Neil 1992).

Incremental Improvement

Such improvements are encouraging, but data that reveal gradual, less dramatic improvement are just as crucial. According to Jay McTighe, director of the Maryland Assessment Consortium, schools need to adopt the spirit of "kaizen," a Japanese word that connotes an ongoing spirit of concern with incremental but relentless improvement, however small. The cumulative impact of many small improvements is thus dramatic. Wiggins thinks that collecting and analyzing data frequently help capture this incremental improvement. Without such activities, we may overlook crucial trend data and affect teacher morale:

> [Teachers will become] insensitive to small gains, which can lead your staff members to conclude that they can't make any difference, no matter what they do (Wiggins 1994a, p. 15).

We do not always need to see dramatic progress; steady growth is sufficient for providing psychic satisfaction and a sense of forward movement (Csikszentmihalyi 1990). Numbers, with the power for revealing slow but steady improvement, combat the fatalism prevalent in schools. The antidote for this fatalism is feedback—clear, precise indications that we are moving forward and becoming more capable.

Disseminating and Replicating Data

Data add another important but overlooked dimension to improvement efforts and the ability to convey and replicate those methods within or beyond our schools. People are more likely to invest in a program that research has substantiated than in a program that is merely touted as "good" by others. "Good" can mean almost anything.

In the Carolingian empire of the early middle ages, trade blossomed when a common currency was introduced. Data that communicate clearly to a wide range of audiences can be our "common

46 currency"; they make the degree of success or failure intelligible to others—school teams, an entire faculty, and other districts.

Everyone wants to succeed, so the better we communicate and substantiate successes, the more likely others are to adapt or replicate those successes. When we do not attempt to use similar language and data, learning from others becomes increasingly difficult. Common measures of achievement "serve many practical purposes" and "enable us to chart trends in areas that have an impact on everyday existence, to plot progress toward significant goals" (Guthrie 1993, p. 523). Common measures aid not only in reaching long-term goals but also in resolving short-term problems:

> [Common measures] convey complicated information to a wide audience quickly, to reach agreement on controversial issues in a relatively short period of time and...[are] a major asset in plotting and planning (Guthrie 1993, p. 523).

Precision, simplicity, intelligibility—educational conversations need more of these attributes. Of course, we should maintain a healthy skepticism about successes we read and hear about. But doesn't it help to know that those claiming improvement took the trouble to gauge and then communicate the level of success they have had with a strategy or an innovation?

Beyond "Take My Word For It"

A recent article discussed the efficacy of word processors in helping students write better compositions. The article was somewhat helpful, but the most specific evidence it marshaled was that children who typically avoided writing began to write enthusiastically because word processors made them feel as though they were real writers. More precise evidence, such as that measured by a writing rubric or by criteria, would have strengthened the point that word processors are in fact improving student writing. Sometimes, we underestimate the value such data would have for the practitioners we are addressing.

Many innovations have come and gone, based on claims such as one I read recently: "The program works. If you don't believe us, come to _____ and see for yourself." Firsthand observations would be great if we had the time or opportunity. More precise information can save us the trip. A study of the outcome-based movement found that testimonials and narrative descriptions may be inspirational, but they are not a good basis for action (Evans and King 1994).

Educators are hungry for both kinds of details: evidence of exactly how well a method works as well as concrete descriptions of how to make it work. Providing both types helped make *In Search of Excellence* (Peters and Waterman 1982) a landmark book in the history of business literature and probably accounts for two best-sellers published by Phi Delta Kappan. They contained profiles of schools that worked, showing evidence of success and how that success was achieved.

Toward a Sane and Reasonable Accountability

Schools should satisfy a community's reasonable expectation that they provide meaningful information on how they are performing. The community deserves evidence that its schools are acting responsibly and in children's best interest. As Michael Fullan tells us, "accountability and improvement can be effectively interwoven" (Fullan 1991, p. 87). Schools in Clovis, California, have enjoyed an excellent local reputation for quality. Clovis educators take accountability seriously—and in stride. It is not a burden. This growing, 25,000-student district is marked by exceptional relations between teachers and administration and between schools and the community that the schools work closely with. Long before "site-based management" entered educational parlance, community members were involved in both school and district goal-setting, using measurable data on everything from academic to affective gains—even the development of character (Schmoker and Wilson 1993). The cover of a promotional flyer shows the district's focus on accountability:

Quality is a Standard
Quality is a Measurable Goal, Not a Vague Sense of Goodness
Quality is a Result

The Clovis schools demonstrate how to interweave accountability and improvement. Both depend upon using measurement judiciously. Data make goals meaningful; without data, we will have only the semblance of accountability.

Parents, communities, and local employers want to know not only about a school and its programs but also how well the school is doing. Here in Amphitheater, we display a question on coffee cups, on posters in buildings around the district, and in a prominent place in the board room. It originated with our special education director, John Rose:

WHAT do we want for our children, and
HOW do we know if we are getting it?

That question has a reasonable expectation: It presumes that schools, like other organizations, have an obligation to communicate clearly to stakeholders and to teachers how they are doing.

Accountability and Professionalism

Linda Darling-Hammond (Darling-Hammond and Goodwin 1993) is convinced that in key respects, teaching has not yet attained the goals of a profession; therefore, it lacks professional status. Among the prerequisites for a genuine professionalism is "accountability, including the relationship that exists between practitioners and their clients and between practitioners and the society at large" (p. 22). We are not there yet.

If schools, like hospitals, fail to serve their clients by failing to institute the most effective methodologies, then the schools should inform the community. Providing such information is a professional obligation. If, on the other hand, schools systematically and continuously adapt the best that is known and are getting good results, they deserve credit and additional support, which will produce even better results. Accountability should place obligations on the schools as well as on the communities that support them. It may be the necessary price to pay for autonomy: "You cannot have *yin* without *yang*. When it comes to the redesigning of America's public schools, you cannot have freedom without accountability" (Fiske 1992, p. 237).

The Common Sense of Teamwork, Goal Setting, and Data Use

When the three concepts of teamwork, goal setting, and data use interact, they address a misunderstanding prevalent in schools. The misunderstanding is that we can improve without applying certain basic principles: People accomplish more together than in isolation; regular, collective dialogue about an agreed-upon focus sustains commitment and feeds purpose; effort thrives on concrete evidence of progress; and teachers learn best from other teachers. We must ensure that these three concepts operate to produce results.

Do we want schools to continue merely adopting innovations? Or do we want schools to improve? Do we want to merely train personnel in new standards and current methodology? Or do we want to help more students apply mathematical operations; write quality essays; deliver effective oral presentations; and appraise and respond to social, historical, and scientific issues? If we collectively focus on such goals and regularly measure the impact of the methods we are learning from each other, we *will* get better results.

4

Rapid Results:
The Breakthrough
Strategy

Educators should take comfort from the fact that we can change the whole organization and how it does business— and we can do so quite rapidly.

—Joyce, Wolf, and Calhoun 1993

The "small, tangible steps" route to strategic breakthroughs is the only implementation strategy I know of that continually delivers dramatic results.

—Peters 1987

Make sustained, rapid improvement a way of life.

—Brian Joiner

Chapters 1–3 discussed the three concepts that are the foundation for improvement: teamwork, goal setting, and the use of performance data. This chapter translates these concepts into key strategies for making the foundation work—and work fast. The "breakthrough strategy" focuses on small but immediate improvements and operationalizes and accelerates the effectiveness of teamwork, goals, and data (Schaffer 1988).

If we consistently analyze what we do and adjust to get better, we will improve. School improvements are neither so "exotic, unusual, or expensive that they are beyond the grasp of...ordinary schools" (Clark et al. 1984, p. 59). But this plan hinges on our ability to see the impact of what we are doing. And that impact does not need to be dramatic; continuous, incremental improvements are the

49

50   real building blocks of sweeping systemic change that is rapid—and attainable.

Most school improvement efforts do not take the "short view" I advocate in this chapter. But some do:

• George Westinghouse Vocational and Technical School in downtown Brooklyn reduced the number of students failing every class from 151 to 11—in *one semester.* Teachers reduced class cutting 39 percent—in *six weeks.*

• The transformation of the Johnson City School District began with Superintendent John Champlin's intense efforts at one school. Achievement gains at this school were evident at the end of *one year.*

• At Hawthorne Elementary School, located in a disadvantaged area of Seattle, 32 percent of African American students were achieving in the lowest quartile (the lowest-achieving 25 percent) in 1989. *One year later,* the number was reduced to 19 percent. During that same period, white students in the lowest quartile went from 8 percent to zero (Bullard and Taylor 1993).

• At the University of California at Berkeley, minority students routinely performed at the bottom of their class in college algebra. A teacher, Philip Treisman, set out to improve their grades. He arranged for them to begin meeting to study and assist each other. Their performance *immediately* improved, exceeding their nonminority counterparts in one semester (Steele 1992).

• At Amphitheater Middle School, a new intervention policy was introduced to reduce the number of disciplinary incidents. At the end of *one 9-week quarter,* 95 referrals had been written; at the same time the previous year, 250 have been written.

• At La Cima Middle School in our district, teacher teams developed and used high-interest activities and assessments to help prepare students to succeed on the state writing exam. In *four months,* La Cima, with its 42 percent free and reduced-lunch population, tied the most affluent school district in Arizona on the state writing exam.

• At Fort Pitt Elementary School in urban Pittsburgh, only 1 percent of 4th graders and 3 percent of 5th graders scored at or above the national norm on the Metropolitan Writing Exam. After teachers adopted a high-engagement, "guided-inquiry" approach to research projects, writing levels rose to 30 percent in 4th grade and to 50 percent in 5th grade—in *one year.* During the same year, discipline referrals plummeted by 71 percent (Hartmann, DeCicco, and Griffin 1994).

• The North Carolina Project adopted new science materials and teaching methods to make science more engaging and hands-on.

Student satisfaction with science classes rose from 38 to 87 percent—
in *one year* (O'Neil 1992).

- Highly successful, early-intervention programs, such as Reading Recovery and Success for All, begin to see results almost immediately. Most improvements in reading occur during the *first semester* of implementation and are often most dramatic during the *first and second years* (Slavin et al. 1994).

- In Israel, a study compared history achievement for two groups. The experimental group was taught using a collaborative/group investigation model; the control group continued to be taught using conventional "whole-class" methods. The result: the experimental group achieved gains *two and half times* that of their whole-class counterparts; they even exceeded the performance of the more advantaged group—in *one year* (Joyce, Wolf, and Calhoun 1993, p. 66).

In each of these cases, schools established collective goals, tracked them using data, then used the data to assess or adjust efforts toward better results. These are the essential ingredients we examined in the first three chapters.

But these rapid successes also reflect judiciously selecting goals that can be reached in a reasonable time. An intensive, collaborative focus on selected goals increases the chance for immediate impact. Joyce, Wolf, and Calhoun (1993) found that "where significant improvement has happened, it has happened rapidly.... Innovations can be implemented and gains seen in student achievement within a year." They insist, in what sounds presumptuous if not heretical in today's climate, that the key is to "pay attention to already existing approaches that work and work fast" (p. 52).

Good News: Room for Improvement

Historically, the quality of education in the United States has been among the best in the world. We have provided an education to record numbers of students over time. But this accomplishment may obscure the current need and opportunity to improve. Although we work hard, we must remember Deming's admonition that "it is possible and in fact fairly easy for an organization to go downhill even though everyone in the organization performs with devotion" (Deming 1986, p. 26). Our educational system fails to work "smarter, not harder," thus limiting improvement opportunities.

Like most organizations, U.S. schools can improve without adding another minute to the school day. Schaffer (1988) explains the reasoning behind this statement by making a radical assumption:

52 Most organizations are only performing between 40 and 60 percent of their capacity.

My experience as an English teacher supports this assumption. During seven years of teaching, I regularly assigned writing activities and required that students read and discuss a variety of texts. But I did little to encourage what could have improved their writing ability: establishing writing criteria and offering opportunities for prewriting, peer editing, and immediate feedback. And I also wasted time by meticulously grading papers that weren't even going to be revised and by scribbling extensive notes over the papers. These practices were ineffective—even harmful (Marzano and Arthur 1977). As a teacher, I was probably operating at 40 to 60 percent capacity—if that.

Unfortunately, my experience was not isolated; most classrooms lack even the most basic teaching processes crucial to good writing (Rothman 1992b). This lack may help explain what the most recent National Assessment of Educational Progress report on student writing found: "No more than 3 percent of students at any grade level were able to write an 'elaborated' or better response" (Olson 1994a). About 73 percent of 4th grade writing samples received low ratings (Jones 1995).

If we had spent even 20 minutes of our monthly department meetings discussing research on what good writing should be, or which methods promoted good writing, many feckless practices might have been replaced with more effective (not to mention time-saving) methods.

The English department at Amphitheater High School exemplifies how teachers can combine teamwork, goals, and data to operate at their capacity. Their efforts have been steadily improving the quality of student introductions in written work. Department members meet regularly to identify and track key difficulties students are having and then share and generate new interventions and materials to help students move toward their goal of becoming better writers. Our new efforts imply a collective goal—to increase the quality of student writing and the number of students who can produce it. The absence of such a goal will keep us from performing at our capacity.

There is room for improvement in a number of areas, which the following examples illustrate:

• **Science**. The science curriculum and textbooks cover almost three times more topics than those of our international counterparts (Olson 1994b). Science texts are dull, emphasizing too much vocabulary and memorization. This approach guarantees shallow coverage. "Despite calls for curricular reforms that emphasize 'doing' science, lectures and textbook use continue to dominate science instruction" (Rothman 1992a, p. 15). We should not be surprised then that most students find high school biology "boring or irrelevant" (*ERS Bulletin* 1990, p. 4).

- **Math.** Research on a national math test reveals that only 18 percent of 4th graders, 25 percent of 8th graders, and 16 percent of 12th graders can perform at the "proficient" level (O'Neil 1993). Another study found "a huge gap" between the new National Council of Teachers of Mathematics (NCTM) standards and "the world of classroom practice" (West 1992, p. 15).
- **Inadequate Teacher Induction.** In Japan and Korea, the law requires that new teachers spend about 20 days during their first year learning the art of teaching from a mentor teacher. In the United States, "supervised induction to teaching is ad hoc or nonexistent" (Darling-Hammond and Goodwin 1993, p. 33).
- **Underfunded Staff Development.** School districts typically spend less than 1 percent of their annual budget on training (Bullard and Taylor 1993). Underfunding at the school level reflects what Deming found on a broader scale: "In its underuse and abuse of talent, America is the most underdeveloped country in the world" (1986, p. 6).
- **Lack of Student Engagement.** Lounsbury and Clark (1990) conducted a nationwide study of 162 middle schools. Years into the middle school movement, which emphasized active learning, they observed a "dominance of passive learning." Most 8th graders "have resigned themselves to the fact that classes are boring" (pp. 136–137). Although we know that students must be engaged in learning to retain and apply it (Wolfe and Sorgen 1990, Newmann 1992), we continue to provide the least engaging kind of curriculum for rural and inner-city students who need the most help (Haberman 1990).
- **Poor Instructional Leadership.** Less than 10 percent of school principals are "systematic problem solvers" (Leithwood and Montgomery 1986). Studies of school leadership show that "the average school administrator...simply reflects on lesser things than the purpose of schooling and curriculum and instruction issues" (Smith and Andrews 1989, p. 4).
- **No Criteria or Expectations Given to Students.** We have discovered that students perform better when we provide them with the criteria we expect them to meet and give them models, examples, and "anchor papers" that specify our expectations (Hillocks 1987, Wiggins 1994a, Stiggins 1994). As Sizer (1992), Wiggins (1994a), and Stiggins (1994) have been telling us, this area is a huge and overlooked opportunity for us to improve.
- **Failure to Reach Children in Poverty.** Only 11 percent of all districts nationwide disaggregate student data to determine how to raise the achievement of the lowest-achieving populations (Bullard and Taylor 1993). We do not address the dismaying fact that, gener-

54

ally, students from low socioeconomic categories are still performing well below their peers. The reason is not solely socioeconomic conditions. Unfortunately, those who teach in rural and urban areas continue to use retrograde and ineffective instructional methods that are not based on research (Haberman 1990).

The problems in these areas point to a large gap between what we know and what we do. How wide is this gap? Joyce, Wolf, and Calhoun (1993) provide some idea:

> Of the 20 or more most powerful teaching strategies that cross subject areas and have a historical track record of high payoff in terms of student effects, we speculate that fewer than 10 percent of us—kindergarten through university level—regularly employ more than one of these strategies (p. 38).

Based on his studies, Edmonds (1979) concludes that "there isn't a single educational problem that doesn't have a solution"; "we can, wherever and whenever we choose, successfully teach all children whose schooling is of interest to us" (p. 23). We can close the gap between what we know and what we do by improving incrementally:

- Increase the number of students who can write—and enjoy writing—quality persuasive essays.
- Increase our staff development budget from the current ½ to 1 percent. Even that additional ½ percent, properly targeted, can make a difference.
- Ensure that relevant and engaging learning occurs with increasing frequency.
- Create expectations and promote training and conditions that help principals focus more time and energy on helping solve the most pressing school problems—one at a time.
- Increase the number of low-achieving students who can achieve at higher levels.

Schools may have more potential for immediate improvement than many other organizations. Why? Because, as outlined in Chapter 3, they suffer from the most crippling weaknesses: They are uniquely cellular, goal-averse, and dataphobic—more so than perhaps any other kind of organization (Lortie 1975, Rosenholtz 1989).

The Need for a Breakthrough: Doing More with What We Have

Such opportunities for improvement make Schaffer's breakthrough strategy especially applicable to schools. It helps clarify what some have known for years: There is a marked difference between vague, well-intentioned improvement efforts and carefully targeted, goal-oriented, short-term efforts aimed explicitly at getting measurable, *substantive* results quickly. The former characterizes the disappointing failures of the past; the latter can achieve better short-term and long-term results. This strategy requires leadership that any dedicated administrator can provide; it does not require immediate and vast increases in resources.

Although change is always "resource-hungry" (Fullan 1991, p. 64), resources can be found as well as made. If we can achieve better results by making better use of what we have, we can make a more compelling case for additional funding. For one thing, new money seldom raises achievement, a pattern that is obvious to the public (Odden, Monk, Nakib, and Picus 1995). Bill Clinton believes that people in the United States are ready to spend more money on education. But they want "some assurance that they are not pouring money down a bottomless hole" (Clinton, in Fiske 1992, p. 276). Because most schools are so poorly organized for improvement, we can use existing resources and personnel to achieve more. Employees at every level are usually convinced that they are producing as much as anyone can with existing resources (Schaffer 1988). But as business and education studies have shown, we can do better.

The 40 to 60 percent assumption is Schaffer's (1988) bedrock principle and defines the opportunity implicit in the breakthrough strategy. He defines the strategy:

> Locating and starting at once with the gains that can be achieved quickly, and then using those first successes as stepping-stones to increasingly ambitious gains (p. 13).

Among the most promising and enlightened school reform movements of the last decade is the Coalition of Essential Schools. Now, many years into its reform effort, the movement appears to be moving slower than originally anticipated. An article in *Phi Delta Kappan* gave a somber assessment of the movement's progress by concluding that "there are no quick fixes or miracle cures. For all their high hopes that it would be 'the reform that's going to make the difference,'" the coalition now "would like to temper this enthusiasm" (Muncey and McQuillan 1993, p. 487). Plenty of process, plenty of time. But not much in the way of results.

Or consider Al Shanker's (1994) frustrated take on school reform in Chicago. Shanker, who is president of the American Federation of Teachers, was eager to see how their schools were progressing. After seven years of school reform, school officials there told him that new initiatives "were making a tremendous difference." He arrived to find

56

"no data or discussion about student performance," only "enthusiastic quotes from students and teachers." He concluded that Chicago's primary problem is that after all these years, the district never made any real "attempt to measure progress toward the goal of improved student achievement and an analysis of what seems to be working and what seems to be failing" (p. 43).

These efforts are not failing for lack of intelligence, effort, or industry. The problem may be that we are too patient. We could be seeing steady, palpable progress, as measured by any number of viable assessments and indicators and by setting a limited number of substantive but realistic short-term goals.

Impatience Is a Virtue: The Importance of Short-Term Goals

In "results-driven programs,…the mood is one of impatience. Management wants to see results now, even though the change process is a long-term commitment" (Schaffer and Thomson 1992, p. 83). This reconciliation between short-term and long-term goals is not what we hear and read about in most education literature. Instead, we are told to avoid an impatient, quick-fix mentality.

Many in the TQM movement were quick to adopt the view that we must "go slow to go fast." This is good advice, because it urges us to prepare adequately, to be thorough and democratic, and to carefully analyze problems as we plan for improvement. But somehow we interpreted such advice to mean that we should not measure progress or establish goals in the beginning. Some exhorted us only to engage in dialogue about processes, excluding results.

Immediately focusing on processes as they affected results was at the core of the success that effective TQM companies experienced. The stories contained in journalist Mary Walton's books (1986, 1990) on measurably successful TQM efforts attest to this focus. Brian Joiner, Deming's close associate, also urges us to "make sustained, rapid improvement a way of life."

Nonetheless, for most business consultants, it was "near-anathema to suggest any focus on results" (Brigham 1994, p. 22). Business people still hear that slowness is a virtue and that results will automatically accrue if companies adopt TQM philosophy and practices—and have patience (Brigham 1994).

Education bought into this misunderstanding. It seemed logical enough; many times in the past, we had sought improvement through such activities as trying new initiatives and new routines. When no results came time after time, we began to examine whether change could or should be expected to come quickly. We concluded that since we took a long time to get into a mess, we would need a long time to get out. We decided it was foolish to expect a quick fix;

real change is deep, systemic, and cultural. And so we gave up on short-term expectations of change.

But short-term planning and measurement promote the successes that add hope to the apparent futility of large-scale reform attempts. Short-term success, even "purposeful impatience," sustains the essential interest and energy to persevere (Fullan 1991, p. 83). Not to mention that short-term, incremental gains are eminently achievable.

Psychological Benefits of Short-Term Results

The most effective TQM companies are obsessed with short-term results—and they get them. Evidence and case studies show that schools can also improve rapidly. Impatience is central to this improvement; patience overlooks a psychological need for feedback, a need that is seldom met in today's workplace. Employees "perceive their psychic rewards to be scarce, erratic, and unpredictable" (Lortie 1975, p. 212). This situation may help explain why "disenchantment is rampant" among veteran teachers, who constitute about 70 percent of the teaching force (Evans 1989, p. 10).

We underestimate the importance of urgency and how fast it dissipates after the initial fanfare. Chang, Labovitz, and Rosansky (1992) think that we should "demand short-term results," and that impatience can be used to our advantage:

> In the real world people aren't very patient. They find it difficult to work hard at something when they're told the results won't be visible for months or even years. That's why we advise our clients to demand short-term results from their long-term TQM process. We advocate what we call the "Quick-Start" Approach (p. 102).

If we want to improve, then we need positive, short-term feedback. Even though "certain activities require a very long time to accomplish,...the components of goals and feedback are still very important" (Csikszentmihalyi 1990, p. 55). Reaching short-term goals provides "joy," which once experienced, makes us want more (Csikszentmihalyi 1990, p. 42). Anticipating short-term benefits energizes the improvement process and keeps it from bogging down in easier, more conventional activities that do not directly affect student results.

Activity-Centered Programs Versus Results-Driven Programs

Educators tend to postpone a concern with ends—with results— perhaps because "means-end relationships in teaching are not well

58

understood" (Lortie 1975, p. 212). Such action is painfully apparent at many educational conferences, where we hear cursory or clichéd descriptions of activities conducted, partnerships formed, and committees established, without any reference to a single result. This endless train of preparation and activities has been called the rain dance:

> [The rain dance is] the ardent pursuit of activities that sound good, look good, and allow managers to feel good—but in fact contribute little or nothing to bottom-line performance. These activities, many of which parade under the banner of "total quality" or "continuous improvement"...[reflect] a fundamentally flawed logic that confuses ends with means, processes with outcomes (Schaffer and Thomson 1992, p. 80).

Compare this definition to a recent description of the dismal state of high school reform, where after more than a decade, "there is a lot of activity but there is not a clear vision as to what is necessary....We're not making much progress" (Viadero 1994, p. 1).

As we have seen, Glickman (1993) discovered that activities can become the goal. In other words, many organizations are "equating measures of activities with actual improvement of performance" (Schaffer and Thomson 1992, p. 84). Such measures have a legitimate use, but not when they ignore student learning results.

"Perpetual Preparations": A Waste of Time and Money

Our patience may be well intended, but it is wrong headed for us to accept long periods of training, restructuring, and activity. "Perpetual preparations" are not only ineffective, they also "waste billions" (Schaffer 1988, p. 39). In the name of patience, many initiatives get so bogged down in endless planning that they "have disappeared in the implementation" (Joyce, Wolf, and Calhoun 1993, p. 6).

I had a conversation with a consultant who had worked intensively with a number of schools for several years. "Any results?" I asked her.

"Oh no," she replied. These efforts are "still evolving." It was "much too early to expect results." Even, I asked her, for the schools where she had worked for three or more years?

"It's premature," she said. They are still "laying the foundation."

Another telling example is one state's 6-year-old reform effort. Even though much expense and activity went toward establishing site-based school councils, the new performance-based assessment program "resulted in only modest changes in teachers' instructional practices." One review found that the "vast majority of teachers" were "frozen in virtually the same instructional patterns" (Guskey 1994, p. 53). Another review found that "the idea that the ultimate purpose of councils is to advance student learning has not been stressed enough" (David 1994, p. 711).

If we set out to establish site councils, we will establish site councils; we will not improve schools.

If we set specific goals and honestly and systematically commit ourselves to achieving them, we will almost invariably improve.

From Early Momentum to Systemic Change

The preceding examples are not the exception; they are the rule. Current organizational habits that avoid focusing on short-term, measurable gains are the major obstacles impeding not only isolated improvements but also systemwide transformation. Palpable gains are the key to leveraging change in the system because they can unravel the "tangle of debilitating patterns that are reinforced by formal and informal institutional mechanisms" (Schaffer 1988, p. 19). Impatience itself can begin to transform the system. Lee Iaccoca once directed his staff to develop a prototype for a convertible. When they enthusiastically responded that they could have one in about nine months, he bellowed, "You just don't understand. Go find a car and saw the top off the damned thing" (Iaccoca, in Peters 1987, p. 253).

Schaffer (1988) cites the example of Domino Sugar, where in just six weeks, problem-solving teams reduced bag breakage by 80 percent and overfill by 56 percent. They achieved the reductions by multiplying brainpower through team problem solving, not by adding resources. This one improvement led to systemwide changes in every department in the refinery.

It also changed the system. Based on these reductions, the improvement was implemented at other plants, where it produced results and also broke down age-old barriers between union and management. Initial skepticism gave way to enthusiasm and cooperation: At first "no one really wanted to own the project—that is until we started to get results. Then everyone got excited and wanted to get into the act" (Schaffer 1988, p. 107).

"Early momentum can mean the difference between a rapid sequence of successes that sustains momentum and a mere plodding along...and no palpable excitement." The need for early, rapid successes indicates that "pilot projects that are selected during the

60   planning stages must have high probability for quick success and meaningful impact" (Brigham 1994, pp. 45–46). It is crucial that we carefully establish concrete, achievable "short-term subgoals." Otherwise, people are unrealistically expected to "maintain a high effort as they slog toward goals they can only attain months or even years later." Such work "may afford team members only a single reinforcing moment of success" (Schaffer 1988, p. 31).

Lortie (1975) saw this 20 years ago: A teacher who felt pride because all her students could read by the end of the year, remarked that "the rest of the year I'm wondering" (p. 127). Quarterly or semester assessments can reveal incremental success as well as feedback that can promote even better annual results.

"Quick Wins in Target Areas"

The key in the early going is to select the right projects. According to an A.T. Kearney report, newcomers applying TQM should select pilot projects that "promote early successes on substantial issues" (Brigham 1994, p. 46). Schaffer and Thomson (1992) maintain that success starts with identifying "quick wins in target areas...initiatives that employees could take right away to generate measurable improvement in a short time" (p. 88). They describe, for instance, a chart on the wall of a microfilm department, revealing the number of missed deadlines. The goal was to honor microfilm requests in 24 hours. After just a few weeks, the chart showed that missed deadlines were going down. Subsequently, "everyone took pleasure in seeing it, and work went forward with renewed vigor" (p. 86).

How can we emulate this success in education? We can select substantive slices—small but meaningful challenges that promote success and hence optimism. As we have seen, in only one year, Centennial Elementary School saw dramatic improvements in students' writing ability. But more important, grade-level teams began to see improvements at the beginning, during monthly meetings.

In Amphitheater, a new optimism is emerging among teacher teams. Using rubrics and other meaningful indicators, our teams have realized rapid, measurable improvements in many areas:

- writing
- research papers
- introductions to essays
- math problem solving
- reading
- descriptive story settings
- oral presentations
- student discipline and responsibility

They are succeeding because they set "conservative goals," which have a near-certainty of being met (Peters 1987, p. 513). Not all schools or departments can "improve writing quality" in a month. But almost any focused, collegial effort that shares best strategies and implementation ideas can succeed in getting more students to write better introductions or better substantiate and defend a thesis with apt illustrations and supporting details—or other building blocks to better writing.

Writing is an excellent place to begin improving. It is an essential interdisciplinary skill, and rubrics for assessing writing are probably familiar to most teachers.

Too Many Goals!

Our zeal to improve may lead to one of the gravest mistakes we can make: taking on more than we can manage. Educational and organizational literature is rife with warnings against this tendency:

• Schaffer (1988) warns against the organizational tendency to "set too many goals...covering too many bases" (p. 29).
• Chang, Labovitz, and Rosansky (1992) offer a recommendation: The number of targeted breakthroughs [should be] explicitly limited to safeguard against all organizations' universal tendency to pursue too many objectives at once (p. 112).
• Joyce, Wolf, and Calhoun (1993) insist that we be "parsimonious about the number of initiatives that are on the table at any time" (p. 44).
• Fullan (1991) warns that attempting too many initiatives at one time can result in "massive failure" (p. 71).
• Hopkins (1994) observes that "successful schools set priorities for development that are few in number" (p. 185).

Because time is arguably a school's most precious and scarce commodity, we cannot afford to waste it on too many goals. Improvement requires time for planning, training, and constructive dialogue. Donahoe (1993) cites schools that schedule improvement sessions at the beginning of the year for each school goal. Adding a goal requires the consent of the entire staff. If a goal is added, one must be removed. Collective times are "concentrated on a limited number of strategies" and "rigorously allocated to specific aspects of the school's agenda" (pp. 304–305).

Our superintendent, Richard Wilson, requires each school to establish only two goals; the second can be a subset of the first. For each goal, a school must schedule six to nine sessions throughout the year for dialogue, data analysis, and improvement planning. In our

62

district, we have seen how easily school councils can generate a long list of objectives that spread efforts too thin, without resulting in any significant accomplishment.

Joyce and his colleagues (1993) found that successful teams meet regularly to discuss progress toward goals: weekly, monthly, or quarterly. Schools in our district meet four to six times a year. With that number of meetings, teachers cannot meaningfully analyze progress and generate improvement ideas for more than a few initiatives, especially at first. For Joyce, a school may want to delay initiatives until it can "afford" the time and other resources to implement them properly (p. 38). One way we can make effective use of short meetings is seen in the Appendix.

A Caveat

Now it *is* conceivable that a high school or middle school could have a number of different goals—for each department. And in some cases, an elementary school may decide to have different goals at different levels—for example, two at primary and two at intermediate. The name of the game is to have each employee involved in no more than a limited number of goals that require the kind of regular time commitment, data analysis, and strategy sessions necessary for success.

A school can also establish minor or related goals, which create focus and concerted effort without needing regular meetings to discuss them. Brief references to successful strategies or progress might be tucked into existing faculty meetings. The following are examples of minor goals for which data can be easily gathered. Such process data can heighten awareness and opportunities for celebration and create a sense of progress that feeds the major academic or behavioral goals pursued:

• The number of disciplinary incidents, with comparisons to last year at the same time.
• Grade-point or rubric data for an important task or ability.
• The percentage of work or assignments students complete.
• The number of teachers completing important training.
• The number of books students read.
• The number of teachers involved in mutual observation for professional improvement.

One of the greatest dangers to a successful improvement effort is losing focus, which results from trying to take on more goals than we have the time and resources to realistically achieve. Schools are under

enormous pressure to respond to every concern their constituents
raise. Among the hardest decisions a school community must make
is to decide democratically which goals reflect the school's highest
priorities—and which it must pursue later. Leaders and facilitators
must be prepared to help their faculties and communities exercise
discipline and take advantage of such useful tools as weighted or
rank-order voting.

Expanding our Vision of What's Possible: The Need for "Zest"

The small starts I describe in this chapter are the seeds of
large-scale success. Small, measurable successes, achieved annually,
quarterly, or monthly, can release the optimism and enthusiasm—or
"zest"—as Schaffer (1988, p. 52) calls it, that may be the most
important ingredient in improvement. The breakthrough strategy
uses this zest to maintain energy for reaching goals, removing barriers, and increasing confidence:

> The breakthrough strategy attempts to recreate the zest fac-
> tors—which release so much force and energy in reaching
> important short-term goals—and uses them as the wedge to
> break through institutionalized barriers. Immediate successes
> are essential if people are to increase their confidence and
> expand their vision of what is possible (p. 60).

Amphitheater Superintendent Richard Wilson likens the impact
of such success to athletic victories. The difference is that "careful
planning can all but ensure small-scale victories. Those victories
provide positive reinforcement. With each small win, a team can
begin to feel like it is unstoppable—like a steamroller—as each success
feeds on itself."

Can we routinely expect such swift and significant change? The
answer is a surprising "yes." The key is to regularly marshal collective
intelligence and chart progress toward goals that teachers have agreed
upon and that can reveal incremental progress. Established performance rubrics provide such ways. I explore these and other possibilities in Chapter 7.

An atmosphere charged with progress and results sustains and
energizes people toward effective alternatives to their existing routines. Myriad organizations, schools, and psychology show that the
process works.

As we have seen, carefully selected, short-term projects can
precipitate successful change—and optimism. Much of what ac-

64

counts for this success is learning about the best that others have studied and discovered. Research, the accumulated, practical knowledge that has been gathered over the last few decades, gives us an added advantage as we seek effective, rapid change. It steers us away from discredited (and therefore time-wasting) practices, while directing us toward what works. The next chapter explores the role of research in the improvement scheme.

5

Research

What we have learned about teaching and learning in the last 15 years is among the most exciting discoveries of our 200-year history.

—Peter Senge

The principles discussed in the preceding chapters were the result of research—formal studies that demonstrate the effectiveness of these principles. But research is not enough; for every item of research we adopt, we must conduct on-site action research. The research we do at the local level is what makes formal, outside research work. Outside research cannot be installed like a car part—it has to be fitted, its effects studied so that we can make needed adjustments.

Nonetheless, until we begin to routinely respect and respond to the best that is known about effective teaching and organizational improvement, we forfeit the benefits of the rich knowledge base that can inform our teamwork as we pursue substantive goals. Until we routinely consult this knowledge base, we limit every student and teacher in our system.

In this chapter, I focus on the importance of good, formal, external research by identifying a few concrete interventions and opportunities that research has shown to have promise. I selected them because they are (1) so potent and (2) currently ignored. When we begin to more systematically close the gap between what we know and what we do, we will be on the cusp of one of the most exciting epochs in the history of education. Most dedicated educators acknowledge this gap, which may be one of the reasons that teaching is still regarded as "the not-quite profession" (Goodlad, in Darling-Hammond and Goodwin 1993, p. 20). As we have seen, Joyce and others (1993) speculate that only the smallest fraction of the best that we know is used routinely by educators from kindergarten through graduate school. Fullan (1994) uses an oxymoron to describe a teacher: a "nonreading professional"; many practitioners do not read what leaders in their field write (p. 246). I am always surprised by the number of teachers in graduate classes I have taught who have never read or heard of publications like *Educational Leadership* or *Phi Delta*

66   *Kappan.* In such a research-poor context, isolated experience replaces professional knowledge as the dominant influence on how teachers teach (Little 1990).

A kind of pseudo-research has rushed into this breach: reforms that were supposedly informed by research and that promised to dramatically improve the quality of education. But these major reforms, which were implemented on a grand, even nationwide scale, never delivered (Gitlin 1990). We did not hear much evidence that they had achieved results in real-school settings or that students were generally learning more as a result of the reforms. The reforms failed and quietly left the stage. "Research" lost vital currency and increasingly now evokes cynicism.

Yet good research, whether we call it best knowledge or best practice, can unleash a vast, dormant potential for making every child's and teacher's life richer and more interesting. Unfortunately, we do not always apply what research shows, as the examples that follow illustrate:

- **Brain Research.** People learn and retain information only when knowledge has relevance and meaning for them. For instance, learners have to perceive that drill and memorization (the kinds that are necessary in math and foreign language classes) are clearly connected to something beyond the drill itself (Caine and Caine 1991, Wolfe and Sorgen 1990). We routinely violate this principle.
- **Basic Skills and Higher-Order Skills.** We also labor under the incorrect notion that students must master basic skills before they can learn higher-order skills or engage in complex activities. Studies in math, reading, and writing clearly demonstrate that the opposite is true: Students learn best when basic skills are taught in a vital, challenging context that makes the skills meaningful. The very thing that keeps students from achieving in these areas is the dry, irrelevant teaching strategies we often employ, especially with students who most need real challenges (Means, Chelemer, and Knapp 1991). Low-performing students stand to gain the most from approaches that incorporate basic skills into complex, higher-order tasks and problems. Schools and effective programs have demonstrated that standardized test scores can improve significantly when challenging tasks and activities are used (Resnick, Bill, Lesgold, and Leer 1991; Schmoker and Wilson 1993; Livingston, Castle, and Nations 1989; Pogrow 1988, 1990).
- **Writing.** The complex skill of writing is still taught in a primitive fashion. Despite research showing the importance of regular practice in writing, it still gets short shrift in the classroom. According to the most recent National Assessment of Educational

Progress data, the average student spends about 30 minutes a week on writing (Jones 1995). An alarming number of students are required to write without the benefit of even the most well-established practices supported by research, such as prewriting and revision (Rothman 1992b). A 1995 story commented on the lamentable state of writing instruction by using words from Shakespeare: "If you have tears, prepare to shed them now" (Jones 1995, p. 18). Too many schools continue to substitute inferior activities for actual reading and writing during the large block of time that is devoted to language arts.

• **Reading.** Research shows that reading itself—lots of it—is the most vital and worthy activity for students to engage in to improve their reading ability and test scores (Krashen 1993). Building language instruction around reading and dialogue about that reading (but not excluding phonics and skills instruction) is the best approach, especially after students have learned basic decoding skills (Palincsar and Klenk 1991). Our approach to teaching basic skills does not reflect this research and underestimates the possibilities that we can realize if we adjust our practices.

• **Leadership.** Research in business and education demonstrates that leadership is essential to substantive and enduring progress. Yet the literature reveals a lack of strategic leadership that focuses on improving instruction. Studies point instead to the realities of our current system—one in which a principal's day seldom reflects any meaningful influence on what goes on in the classroom (Smith and Andrews 1989). And principals rarely apply systematic approaches to solving school problems: Only about 10 percent of school principals are "systematic problem solvers" (Leithwood and Montgomery, in Fullan 1991, p. 151). This situation is not the principal's fault. Everyone should be responsible for adjusting the current system to increase opportunities, not just to manage but to lead schools toward ever-improving results.

• **Intervention.** We overlook a growing body of research showing that early, intensive intervention ensures that students can get a good start in school by leaving 1st grade with the ability to read at 1st grade level. Strategies used in intervention programs, such as Success for All and Reading Recovery, succeed because they incorporate word skill strategies and construct meaning from texts. They also insist on the "regular, ongoing assessment" that is advocated throughout this book (Pikulski 1994, p. 17). Research for these early-intervention strategies is so compelling that companies such as Reading Renaissance offer money-back guarantees if schools do not see dramatic results.

• **Socioeconomic Factors and Achievement.** Socioeconomic factors never have and never will preclude high achievement—for

68   groups or individual children. Numerous studies reveal that a *school's* effectiveness is what promotes high achievement (Goodlad 1975). With the right in-class interventions, traditionally low achievers can significantly out-achieve their high socioeconomic (SES) counterparts (Joyce, Wolf, and Calhoun 1993; Steele 1992). In their studies, Mortimore and Sammons (1987) found that in reading, school interventions were "about six times more important than background. For written math and writing, the difference is tenfold" (p. 6). How many ambitious plans have we scrapped, how much teacher morale and human potential have we squandered because we unquestionably bought the notion that socioeconomic factors determined students' level of achievement? We should make discussion of this issue one of our first and highest priorities.

In too many cases, research exerts no influence on what happens in schools. We must address this problem. We must wake up to the opportunity we have to inform practice with vital, practical, professional knowledge. If we are serious about change, we must begin to take advantage of brief opportunities to read and share articles and discuss their implications for action at faculty and administrative meetings, study sessions, and early-out days. Teachers should have opportunities to devote at least part of every summer to such study and to research-based action planning.

Of course, no outside research is complete until teachers conduct their own research on the effects at the school or classroom level. The most important laboratory for change is the local school, where cultural and contextual factors can make or break the success of the most promising and proven procedures. The next chapter explores the richer array of options we now have to assess teaching processes and results and therefore more effectively conduct such local research.

5

Redefining Results

It is time for a more balanced and pragmatic understanding of "results." This redefinition should demystify what happens in schools—for teachers, parents, and students—who need more meaningful indicators of progress and clear descriptions and examples of the kinds of work we want students to be able to do. Test scores and letter grades by themselves do not give us this kind of information. The current revolution in assessment makes a new definition possible—one that includes but is not limited to standardized tests and other traditional assessments.

Beyond Standardized Scores and Dropout Rates

"Results" should take us beyond the exclusive use of such annual indicators as test scores and dropout rates. If we want these to improve (and who doesn't?), we need to focus on the short-term results and feedback that tell us how we are doing in reaching short-term subgoals and long-term goals. Such efforts give us more timely information and a more informative "report card" for the communities we serve. School report cards are still hopelessly narrow, containing little information about student achievement (Jaeger, Gorney, and Johnson 1994) and concealing more than they reveal.

"Results" currently refers to the most limited and remote kind of large-scale, annually assembled data. The problem is that such data do not inform or derive from a teacher's ongoing weekly and monthly efforts. Peters (1987) is *almost* right when he says that "what gets measured gets done" (p. 480). Things get done only if the data we gather can inform and inspire those in a position to make a difference. Information must promote purpose, and the right information must be available to practitioners when they need it.

We must be careful to measure what matters, especially what matters to those who can implement change. We need to analyze not only standardized tests, but also local, teacher-generated assessments; not only bottom-line product or summative scores, but also ongoing process improvement data; not only progress toward long-term objectives, but also progress toward specific short-term or ad hoc subgoals; not only progress toward academic results, but also

70   progress toward behavioral goals that are linked to those results. All these should constitute the new model for assessment and results.

As we have seen, Csikszentmihalyi (1990) discovered that people will not work eagerly and imaginatively toward goals they do not regard as their own. When we judge schools solely on the basis of a few annual, one-size-fits-all measures, we risk alienating practitioners. They know that test scores and dropout rates do not tell the whole story.

Accountability—with a Human Face

We must make sure that accountability focuses on improving results. The information we collect and analyze should help us understand and improve instructional processes that help get better results. Our constituents should be informed of our work so that they know how we are doing and can help us figure out how we can all work together more effectively.

But accountability is difficult to show in the present system. McDonald (1993) provides a telling illustration. Two parents ask how their 14-year-old is doing in middle school. This is, they discover, not a simple request. They need to consult with each of six teachers, who provide anecdotal evidence and grades—both of which can be inflated or which may reflect unpredictable and varying levels of accuracy. Parents want something reliable and objective. The closest thing to reliability and simplicity is standardized test scores—understanding them is easier than trying to negotiate the mysteries of the current reporting system.

By failing to supplement standardized tests with richer, more meaningful alternatives, we unwittingly invite our communities to use only test scores to judge us. We set ourselves up to be judged by an assessment that few of us believe is adequate. The upshot is this weird dance that includes everything from a constructive attempt to improve test scores to outright denial and manipulation of these scores—like we see in connection with the "Lake Wobegon effect"; all the children in every state were found to be above average. Such machinations are hardly the stuff of purposeful, passionate goal-oriented effort. Without abandoning conventional and standardized measures, we have an opportunity to break this game wide open.

Demystifying Results: The Rubrics Revolution

One of the most promising developments in assessment is rubrics, with their capacity to provide useful, quantitative data on clear, carefully selected, *qualitative* criteria. "Rubric" simply means a rule or guide. In education, it's the written criteria—or guide—by which

student performance or a product is judged. Wiggins includes simple   71
criteria lists under this term. The Pomperaug Regional School District
in Middlebury/Southbury, Connecticut, relies heavily on such lists
in every area and a host of assignments. Rubrics can also refer to
descriptions of quality, which are assigned a weighted numeric value
in ascending or descending order. Figure 6.1 shows a rubric for
assessing student writing. Notice how it clearly describes expectations
and how the elements for "3" and "4" papers are similar to descriptions of good writing in general. The difference is that the rubric nails
the criteria down, making them available to schools, teachers, parents, and students and providing clear direction and focus.

FIGURE 6.1

Rubric for Assessing Student Writing

A "4" paper fully addresses the prompt and is written in a style appropriate
to the genre assessed. It clearly shows an appropriate awareness of audience. The
paper "comes alive" by incorporating mood, style, and creative expression. It is
well organized, containing sufficient details, examples, descriptions, and insights
to engage the reader. The paper displays a strong beginning, a fully developed
middle, and an appropriate closure.

A "3" paper addresses the prompt and is written in an appropriate style. It is
probably well organized and clearly written but may contain vague or inarticulate
language. It shows a sense of audience but may be missing some details and
examples. It has incomplete descriptions and fewer insights into characters and
topics. The paper may show a weak or inappropriate beginning, middle, or
ending.

A "2" paper does not fully address the prompt, which causes the paper to be
rambling and disjointed. It shows little awareness of audience. The paper demonstrates an incomplete or inadequate understanding of the appropriate style.
Details, facts, examples, or descriptions may be incomplete. The beginning,
middle, or ending may be missing.

A "1" paper barely addresses the prompt. Awareness of audience may be
missing. The paper demonstrates a lack of understanding the appropriate style.
The general idea may be conveyed, but details, facts, examples, or descriptions
are lacking. The beginning, middle, or ending is missing.

Source: Arizona State Assessment Program, Arizona Department of Education, Phoenix.

Rubrics have many benefits. First, they promote good performance by clearly defining that performance and showing that such
work is achievable. Second, they provide better feedback than the
current system by requiring more precision and clarity about criteria
for evaluating student work (O'Neil 1994). Third, they bring a wel-

72   come end to the disheartening experience we have all had: handing in an assignment without really knowing how the teacher will evaluate it and with no idea of whether the teacher will think it is excellent or shoddy.

No one wants to "fly blind." "Optimal experience" is a direct function of a "goal-directed, rule-bound action system that provides clear clues as to how well one is performing" (Csikszentmihalyi 1990, p. 71). Goals, rules, and clues are what rubrics provide by giving the kind of clarity that is essential to both enjoyment and productivity. George Hillocks (1987) found that merely using scales (another word for rubrics) was among the most significant factors that favored improved writing skills, second only to the quality and design of the writing assignment itself. If we want to maximize their impact, we should be disseminating—even displaying—rubrics everywhere: in schools, classrooms, homes—on refrigerators.

Rubrics can easily and quickly be created or adapted for any task or subject area. An excellent source for explaining how is *Assessing Student Outcomes,* by Marzano, Pickering, and McTighe (1993) and Grant Wiggins's materials in *Standards, NOT Standardization* (1993).

Promoting Learning

As Hillocks (1987) and Csikszentmihalyi (1990) have corroborated, people work more productively if they have clear targets. Using rubrics to establish clear targets has profound implications for educators. We all work more effectively and purposefully toward what we can see and comprehend, and the rules and clues in rubrics enable both teachers and students to understand and hence more effectively work toward higher levels of quality. The levels of achievement the rubrics represent satisfy the psychological need for progress and improvement at every level—for individuals, schools, and districts. The primary value of rubrics is their capacity to provide clear, useful feedback that can be analyzed to identify areas of strength and weakness at any time, at any level, for any number of audiences—from students to whole communities.

Promoting Purpose

Rubrics and criteria provide schools with the opportunity to begin marking improvement and identifying areas for analysis, discussion, and corrective action. We have seen in our district how rubrics and criteria for targets such as the following can be easily developed by teams of teachers in a small amount of time:

• The number or percentage of students who can achieve proficiency levels in writing an effective position paper for social studies, English, and science.

- The number or percentage of students who can achieve the most essential proficiencies in math, with submeasures in such areas as written demonstration, computation, and application.
- The number or percentage of students who can achieve proficiency in musical and artistic performance.
- The number or percentage of students who can achieve proficiency in oral presentations (a skill increasingly acknowledged as essential to future success).

Imagine the possibilities for promoting a sense of organizational and instructional purpose, identifying priorities, and making schools and site councils truly meaningful—in a climate where rubric data reflecting progress toward selected goals are selectively posted and published on charts for discussion. A proliferation of such data and progress charts would serve as constant, visible reminders of a school's truest and highest priorities.

Such an approach enables educators and communities to set the agenda together, based on a broader and richer array of indicators. Again, the good news is that rubrics are underused as part of systematic, goal-oriented improvement efforts; therefore, to the extent that we systematically implement their use, we can redefine results and move toward a better education for more students almost immediately.

Subgoals

The criteria made explicit in rubrics can themselves define the subgoals necessary to attain annual and long-term objectives. The English department at Amphitheater High School developed a common rubric for writing improvement. To promote short-term improvement, teachers focused on introductions and thesis statements as their subgoal. They devised a 3-point rubric for introductions to ensure consistency for teachers and students. The team began sharing effective strategies and materials at their regular meetings. Almost immediately, members began to see and chart improvement. Between October and December 1994, the percentage of students who were writing introductions at or above standard rose from 35 to 53 percent. By May 1995, the number increased to 82 percent. That is breakthrough improvement.

As in politics, all improvement is ultimately local. I do not mean to imply that we should reject state or district requirements; but we must have the opportunity to fashion activities and assessment around what we are learning and observing at the place where improvement matters most: in our own schools and classrooms.

Assessing Subject-Area Content

Rubrics can be especially useful for assessing content mastery, and many are available for this type of assessment (see Marzano,

74   Pickering, and McTighe 1993, pp. 94–95). They encourage what is perhaps the best way of demonstrating such mastery: the essay exam, which can be rubric scored. Essays not only allow students to show knowledge of large amounts of content but also emphasize the *meaning of subject knowledge*, which favors retention. The essay exam should be a part of every teacher's arsenal for teaching and assessing content. Richard Stiggins (1994), an advocate of assessing content knowledge as well as processes and skills, speaks of the "vast untapped potential" of essay assessment (p. 134). As many early 20th century exams reveal, essays assess mastery the old-fashioned way: They promote the critical, higher-order processing of content as they assess mastery of information. Rubrics can help teachers assess such work.

Quizzes and tests serve a vital (and time-efficient) function, too; grades and scores can provide data that we use to derive better, more engaging and effective ways of helping students master material. Objective test results can reveal important information:

- Concepts or content areas that students are having difficulty mastering.
- Knowledge that students don't find arresting or relevant and hence don't retain.
- The need to connect content to life or to a meaningful context.
- The need for review, discussion, or clarification.

As we increase our use of rubrics and performance assessment, improving objective test scores may be an opportunity for getting better results. Once we establish common goals, we should be able to conduct item analyses that reveal useful data:

- The number of students achieving at or above standard (e.g., above a certain percentage) on tests and quizzes.
- The areas of highest and lowest retention of content.

The stage is then set for substantive teacher collaboration, sharing, and brainstorming for more active and engaging ways to teach content and to creatively use or supplement a textbook. Ironically, discussing and analyzing objective test scores can lead us out of some ponderous and unengaging practices. Such activities can take us beyond those bland, rote methods that now hobble us in our attempt to sustain student enthusiasm.

Success from Rubrics

States that use rubrics to assess writing have realized profound improvements. In Maryland, writing rubrics are the heart of a more general improvement effort. The rubrics are sent home to parents and posted in schools and classrooms. Teachers use and adapt them for all disciplines. The result? Over the last decade, Maryland has seen the percentage of students who reach proficiency levels rise from below 47 to above 90 percent, with breakthrough improvements occurring after only one year.

Teachers in the Oak Harbor School District in Washington had an incomplete picture of how well their students were writing. Then they developed a districtwide scoring rubric, which immediately identified deficiencies in every category. The data enabled them to begin systematically addressing the deficiencies. After one year, an outside assessor reported that "remarkable improvements" had occurred and that the new program was a "phenomenal success." The following year those gains were "sustained and improved" (Daniel 1993, p. 44).

An especially inspiring story comes from Colorado's Weld County School District 6. The percentage of students who learned to write at or above the standards on the district writing rubric rose dramatically after the rubric was introduced during the 1988-89 school year (see Figure 3.1 on p. 30). Rubrics defined these standards and thus motivated students from all backgrounds to achieve them (Waters, Burger, and Burger 1995). Under such conditions, what gets measured (and clearly defined) does get done.

Rubrics are becoming increasingly available in all disciplines. But despite an encouraging momentum and growing awareness, teachers do not routinely use them in classrooms. Most districts don't even report writing or other rubric-based performance data to communities. This absence points up yet another huge opportunity. Rubrics may be the catalyst for generating the kind of frequent, focused, measurable improvement and performance data that effectively address professional priorities and the need for accountability.

Demystifying Results with Examples of Excellence

Not all parents and children know what quality work looks like or understand the criteria for it, because few schools provide representative, intelligible examples of what they expect students to strive for (Wiggins 1994b). And finding out the nature of assignments children are given, such as their number, length, and kind—or how many books children are expected to read—is surprisingly difficult for parents. Parents not only want better information about what their children are learning, they want *more of it* (Jaeger, Gorney, and Johnson 1994). We have underestimated this interest. As our economy becomes increasingly knowledge based, look for this attention to increase.

The emerging interest in exemplary student work or anchor papers is especially fortunate. Such examples of excellence clearly

76 exhibit what we want from students. Models and exemplary samples of student work are themselves goals: the clear, concrete expression of the results we wish children to achieve. When accompanied by descriptive rubrics, exemplary student work defines achievement goals in meaningful form.

We should begin displaying, publishing, and referring to models of achievement within and between every area of study. Wiggins (1994a) thinks that posting models or exemplars in schools creates an atmosphere that promotes improvement almost by itself, without administrative coercion. Seeing what children have actually done extends our sense of student potential and defies the limits we might put on children.

A Historic Convergence

We are witnessing a historic convergence of developments: We are creating, using, and disseminating rubrics and other enlightened assessments more; parents want more and better information; and we now recognize that anchor papers and models make desired results less abstract and thus accelerate the ability to learn. Rubric scores have also been found to be increasingly reliable for assessing school improvement efforts. We are getting past the misperception that rubrics scoring is wildly erratic. "Inter-rater reliability" among different evaluators can be as high as 90 percent when the right training is provided. Though still relatively underused, rubrics are gaining ground.

Norm-referenced, standardized scores have their role, but if we take advantage of the moment, the revolution now occurring will add a new dimension to assessment and reporting. Technology is an emerging partner; we can collect, manage, and aggregate data on hand-held computers, which can quickly organize the data to reveal strengths and weaknesses on the skills and proficiencies we choose.

Rubrics are key pieces of this change in assessment, opening up a new world to redefine what counts in schools. Without compromising the qualitative nature of student performance, rubrics enrich and validate quantitative results, even in areas we once thought unmeasurable. No measurement is ever perfect, but rubrics allow us to evaluate more precisely and accurately areas where quality standards have traditionally been ill-defined. Rubrics represent a shift in thinking about how well or reliably we can gauge and assess such intangibles as quality writing, thought, and application. And because they promote the clarity and collective focus that research tells us is essential to improvement, they inevitably favor better results (Rosenholtz 1989, Little 1990).

Are Standardized Tests the Enemy?

The objective emphasis of standardized tests does not have to drive schools toward "drill and kill." Research shows that students who attend schools where subject matter is made relevant and interesting are retaining more and will therefore earn higher scores on standardized tests. This finding indicates that these tests are somewhat useful, especially when we consider the evidence that an abundance of reading, writing, and authentic math experiences is quite possibly the best way to promote success on these tests (Krashen 1993, Resnick et al. 1991). Standardized tests can reveal both progress and areas needing improvement. Without derailing alternative efforts to gauge student performances and higher-order skills, standardized tests can help us make comparative assessments on how well our students are learning basic knowledge and skills. Such tests have been found to be an impressive predictor of future student success. Their statistical reliability is well documented (Walberg, Haertel, and Gerlach-Downie 1994).

Because standardized tests are easy to administer and routinely used, they provide a good "first level of analysis" for people wishing to improve their schools (Bamburg and Medina 1993, p. 36). In a balanced treatment of such tests' worth, Bamburg and Medina found that when used properly, tests can provide the initial leverage for driving many benefits:

> At the school level, the disaggregation [of standardized test data] refocused the staff's purpose, reaffirmed their beliefs, increased the congruence between what was espoused and practiced, focused the instructional conversation, established data-driven priorities, and helped staff affirm that they do make a difference for all children (p. 38).

Using these tests, people such as Effective Schools consultant Larry Lezotte have helped numerous schools see and then address inequities in the quality of education they provide (Bullard and Taylor 1993).

Rubrics and Traditional Assessments: The Best of Both

Schools known for their relevant and enlightened learning activities have also realized exceptional improvement on standardized tests. It is hard to find a school where children are receiving a quality education but where standardized test scores are low.

Teachers at Westwood School in Dalton, Georgia, undertook to depart from the restraints of a test-driven curriculum. They started

78   with mathematics, refashioning the curriculum and orchestrating an
improvement effort that would ensure greater depth, engagement,
and application. In one school year, the spring achievement scores
were *the highest to date* (Livingston, Castle, and Nations 1989). Their
experience is not unique:

• In an inner-city setting, Resnick and her associates set out to
improve student math performance, using "as little school drill
material as possible" to teach math with manipulatives and other
rich, "reasoning-based" methods. In one year, 1st grade math scores
rose from a mean of about the 25th to the 80th percentile. The
following year, mean achievement with the experimental group was
at the 70th percentile (Resnick et al. 1991, p. 47).

• Similarly, many of the accelerated schools, such as Daniel
Webster in urban San Francisco and Hollibrook Elementary School
in Houston, Texas, realized enormous gains on standardized test
scores within two years of departing from drill and kill to more
engaging student learning activities.

• The Coalition of Essential Schools' Central Park East Secondary School in East Harlem, New York, saw gains in test scores when
former Director Deborah Meier and her new faculty came in with a
philosophy that emphasized interactive teaching methods and learning activities: writing workshops, thematic units, discussion, and
inquiry (Schmoker and Wilson 1993).

• According to Stan Pogrow, "The biggest secret in American
education is that at-risk students love to learn and be challenged with
very sophisticated tasks" (1990, p. 62). Pogrow's Higher-Order Thinking Skills (HOTS) program, emphasizing complex tasks and Socratic
questioning and thinking skills, has helped numerous schools get
better results on standardized tests in both reading and math (1988,
1990). At 2,000 school sites in 48 states, the HOTS program has
realized, on average, twice the gains of alternative approaches used
at those same schools; the program has had three times the gains in
reading comprehension. Using this carefully researched, metacogni-
tive approach, 5th graders throughout the Detroit Public Schools
gained 16 months in reading and 13 months in math during the
1994-95 school year. Recent implementation at Elvira Elementary
School in Tucson, Arizona, was successful by several measures. In one
year, standardized scores in reading and math went up 13.5 normal
curve equivalents (NCE), as did writing scores and GPAs, irrespective
of socioeconomic status.

Standardized tests, if disaggregated and thoughtfully analyzed,
can provide feedback and goal-orientation. By themselves, the tests

haven't universally inspired teachers to reach viable goals. They don't sufficiently or frequently enough capture the kind of education we should provide. Unless supplemented by other richer and more precise indicators, they have a limited and possibly an unfortunate influence on instruction and its improvement (Smith 1991; Haladyna, Nolen, and Haas 1991).

The real problem, as Wiggins points out "is not [standardized] tests per se but the failure of classroom teachers…to be results focused and data driven"—to use these results wisely and as part of a wider array of assessments (Wiggins 1994a, pp. 17–18).

Another problem is our failure to report on the results achieved with other assessments, for example, school or district examples of excellence and scores on literary and social studies essays, science performances, and multistep, open-ended math problems. Why not report these? Why not begin making them a part of the public conversation? Schools must take the initiative here.

We must now move toward a new accountability, a new results-orientation, analogous to the baseball card that Wiggins (1994b) uses to illustrate how we should begin marking progress for ourselves, parents, and communities. Win-loss records (like standard grades) are one thing; a baseball card contains *a variety* of significant, specific results, such as stolen bases, batting averages, runs batted in, walks, and strikeouts. Educationally analogous information should be the new norm for education. Like Wiggins's baseball card, the information we gather should enable us to chart and disseminate a richer variety of results. We can thus proclaim the legitimacy of school or district assessments that measure student performance in many areas:

- Musical and artistic performances.
- Quarterly or semester content essay exams.
- Discussion and listening skills.
- Debate and oral presentation skills.
- Student behavior and responsibility.
- Ability to solve multistep math problems and apply math principles.
- Ability to write effective analytical or persuasive papers in social studies and literature.
- Ability to conduct and write up a scientific experiment.

Redesigning Report Cards

If we truly wish to change the way we assess, the report card may be one of the main leverage points. The innovative Key School in Indianapolis provides progress reports for each of Howard Gardner's

80

seven areas of intelligence. The Kyrene School District in Tempe, Arizona, reports student levels of development in three activities not typically assessed on report cards:

- Reads fluently.
- Makes sensible predictions.
- Uses word recognition strategies (i.e., phonics structure and context).

As a parent, I'd *love* to get such information on my daughters. The Tucson Unified School District is piloting a similar report card in 25 schools, which provides rubrics for everything from the traditional content areas to student progress in learning to become a "collaborative worker" and a "self-directed learner." Parents, predictably enough, are giving the report card good reviews (Clarridge and Whitaker 1994).

Wouldn't we like to know how students in state and neighborhood schools are faring in these areas, in addition to the traditional skill and content areas? Then we need to embrace an expanded reporting and assessment system. New report cards that parents, teachers, and the business community design democratically can help promote the kind of education everyone wants for their children.

We must measure and, in some cases, more routinely publicize what is most important and reflects state and local priorities. We need to emphasize the bottom line without rejecting a concern for the processes and subgoal measurements that lead to bottom-line improvements. Such processes and subgoals should continuously be evaluated relative to learning and behaviors that we determine are the primary purpose of schools. Chapter 7 offers specific examples of how we can flesh out this new conception toward getting better results with students in our schools.

7

Opportunities
for Action Within
and Among the
Subject Areas

This chapter suggests options and opportunities for beginning the venture toward results-oriented improvement. While they are not intended to be prescriptive, the options are offered in the confidence that any school or district can implement something similar. The process can be accelerated if we begin to systematically bank and disseminate the best assessments in our schools, districts, and states. To be meaningful, such assessments must be conducted and analyzed not just annually but regularly during the school year.

The discussion assumes that despite the obvious state of ferment in curriculum and assessment, we do not have to succumb to paralysis. We can do much to embrace the best of the past and anticipate and prepare ourselves for the future. We can organize for results now—and we can get them.

The Subject Areas

The current interest in interdisciplinary learning still leaves room for emphasizing the disciplines. As Howard Gardner points out, we must not be in a rush to toss out the disciplinary baby with the bath water; a good grounding in the disciplines is the best basis for interdisciplinary success (Gardner and Boix-Mansilla 1994). Even those who advocate integrating the disciplines have cautioned that for practical reasons, we need to begin with strategies that embrace, rather than diminish, the legitimacy of the disciplines (Ackerman 1989). Frederick County, Maryland, Director of Assessment Steve Hess, who helped found the Maryland Assessment Consortium, recommends that strongly emphasizing application *within* the con-

82   tent areas is the best grounding for authentic integration within and *among* the disciplines. Striking the right balance takes time; we are still finding our way on this journey. In the meantime, consider some possibilities for action that we can take now in specific subject areas.

Social Studies

Educator Walter Parker (1991) believes that social studies is in a state of relative disarray. Grades and credits reflect nothing more than time spent in class and "practically nothing about the abilities and understanding that graduates have or have not achieved" (p. 15). As an antidote, he recommends building a social studies curriculum around benchmark assessments. Sample assessments from Parker and the National History Standards Project are shown in Figure 7.1. As you examine them, consider how easily they can be adapted and administered. Consider, too, how powerfully they can orient social studies teaching toward attaining both content mastery and higher-order intellectual achievement. Teachers can generate assessments like these for every unit of social studies, from history to current issues and events. Discussion and activities can then reinforce and prepare students to succeed on such assessments.

FIGURE 7.1

Sample Benchmark Assessments for a Social Studies Curriculum

At the End of Elementary School

Students write a summary of a current public controversy drawn from school life and tell how a courageous and civic-minded American they have studied (e.g., Sojourner Truth or James Madison) might decide to act on the issue.

At the End of Junior High/Middle School

Students write an analysis of a current public controversy facing their community and draw an historical comparison.

Source: Parker 1991, pp. 24–25.

* * *

Grades 7–12

Analyze the connection between political ideas and economic interests [for a certain nation(s) or historical period(s)] and compare the ideas and interests of different groups.

Source: National History Standards Project.

The Pomperaug Regional School District in Middlebury, Connecticut, has used questions based on topics that the Bradley Commission and the National Geographic Society outlined. Such comprehensive but manageable criteria have generated both wonderful assessments and essential questions for a social studies curriculum. For example, teachers use the following questions for a unit on culture:

- **Grades 5 and 6.** "How does the specific geography and environment influence the development of that culture?"
- **Grades 7 and 8.** "What values, beliefs, political ideas, and institutions have the people of the United States developed?"
- **Grade 11.** "How have geographic factors contributed to the development of regions of the United States? How did these differences fuel the Civil War?"

Such open-ended, "big questions" invite elaborated, interpretive responses that get at content in a meaningful and arresting way. The Australian graduation exams contain similar questions, *without* raising hackles about national versus local preference and control. Such questions allow considerable teacher and student autonomy within a common framework known as the "Common Assessment Tasks." The Australian assessments demonstrate that even national assessments don't necessarily stifle local influence. It *can* be done (Howe and Vickers 1993). Orienting social studies toward such questions promotes a thoughtful, engaging, inquiry-driven treatment of knowledge and content and increases the possibilities for interdisciplinary tie-ins to science and language arts.

Any number of rubrics can be used to evaluate responses to such prompts, including modifying the rubrics we discussed in Chapter 6. A rubric from Marzano, Pickering, and McTighe's book (1993), which is full of excellent rubrics and representative learning activities, is a good example of one that can be adapted for social studies. Figure 7.2 shows Level 4 of the rubric.

FIGURE 7.2

Level 4 of a 4-Point Rubric for Written Assignments

A. Effectively interprets and synthesizes information
    4: Consistently interprets the information gathered for tasks in accurate and highly insightful ways and provides unique syntheses of that information.

Source: Marzano, Pickering, and McTighe 1993, p. 96.

---

84   Short-term subgoals can be developed from part or all of an assessment. For example, teachers can collect and analyze the concrete components of "insightful" responses, then share strategies for improving student capacity for such insights. Improvement efforts involve collecting data on the number of students satisfying the criteria or achieving at a "3" or "4" level—and then determining which will be the most germane interventions for increasing that number.

Results and continuous improvement in the social studies can be simple. Teachers can regularly collaborate to compare, either in general or numerical terms, how students are doing on conventional objective tests and quizzes or on essay exams. Sharing lessons and methods promotes higher scores; sharing unit assessments saves time and promotes a broader, more precise collaboration. As Rosenholtz points out, similarity of goals enables professionals to more capably help each other.

Language Arts and Literature

In the preceding chapters, we examined several cases of improvement in the language arts, specifically in writing. Although all disciplines should stress good written and oral communication, the language arts play an important general role: cultivating the communications skills that are vital to every discipline. But English and language arts have their own domains as well: literature and its understanding. A full education must provide opportunities to ponder, explore, discuss, and analyze the richness of human experience, which novels, poetry, short stories, and poetry afford. In social studies, students can debate the wisdom of the United States entering World War I; in language arts, they can read and discuss the deeper human issues raised in *All Quiet on the Western Front.*

As students begin to read literature insightfully, we can use rubrics to gauge their development. Again, a good source for such rubrics is found in *Assessing Student Outcomes,* by Marzano and others (1993). When we can assess the growth of students' critical reading skills relative to documents like the U.S. Constitution, *The Diary of Anne Frank*, or an editorial on the effects of acid rain, we open the door to meaningful, focused collaboration among teachers.

In addition to rubrics, another good measurement is the number of books students read, which research shows is among the best indicators of student reading development. Stephen Krashen's studies (1993) found that creating conditions conducive to lots of reading promotes everything from vocabulary development to comprehension and writing skills (and higher test scores).

Math   85

Earlier chapters described how teachers can get better results on conventional tests by developing and administering assessments together. Math teachers can apply this principle by scanning test results for strengths and weaknesses and then discussing ways to improve learning. Or, even more effective, they can do an item analysis of collective results, which they submit anonymously, creating a safe, collaborative environment. The obvious advantages are the enormous amounts of time saved and constructive, focused staff development. This collaboration may begin with research-based minilessons that address the most apparent priorities revealed by the study.

Math teachers can collaborate to get better results in higher-order math proficiencies as well. For instance, when all teachers are working from the same math rubric, their conversation can revolve around the common elements and criteria described in that rubric. Figure 7.3 shows Level 4 of a rubric that can be used to assess content, computation, and higher-order mathematical processes. At regular intervals, teachers can discuss student success—or difficulty—on any part of the rubric. A well-organized team can go one step further by charting collective progress on the same assessment at certain intervals to even more precisely observe trends in difficulty or improvement.

FIGURE 7.3
Level 4 of a 4-Point Rubric for Math

Goal: Every student will be able to effectively solve math problems.
    Possible subgoals: Every student will be able to produce solutions that
- Show complete understanding of the problem.
- Thoroughly address all points relevant to the solution.
- Show logical reasoning and valid conclusions.
- Communicate effectively and clearly through writing and/or diagrams.
- Include adequate and correct computations and/or setup.

Source: Adapted from the Arizona State Assessment Program, Arizona Department of Education, Phoenix.

Obviously, mathematics *is* evolving. How do we keep pace with the changes? Consider the National Council of Teachers of Mathematics' (NCTM) statement on algebra, *Algebra for Everyone* (National Council of Teachers of Mathematics 1994). NCTM regrets the current

86   state of teaching algebra "divorced from any natural context" (p. 1). They are calling for a shift from algebra as a set of manipulative skills to algebra as a means of representation. That shift requires that we do more to stress quantitative patterns and relationships as they appear in statistics, shape, and change. All we have to do is add, a few at a time, such problems and components to both instruction and assessment. In some cases, we may need to substitute one problem for another on formative or summative assessments, substituting a multistep or application problem for one that only requires computation. In others, we may need to add a component to an already existing problem—for example, a requirement to provide a written explanation for how to solve the problem. Either way, we can progress, adjust, and meet the future without having to wait indefinitely until the state of the discipline fully settles—which will never happen. We always need to maintain a balance of computation, application, and representation in mathematics.

Science

Science, too, is in a state of ferment. Like math, science has an excessive amount of content to cover, about two to three times as much as in other countries (Olson 1994b). But while we wait for the needed paring of the science curriculum, we can begin getting better results now on both objective tests and alternative assessments and performances.

Shavelson and Baxter (1992) write that "a combination of indicators (e.g., multiple-choice and performance assessments) may be needed to provide a complete picture of achievement" (p. 23). In addition to objective tests, they recommend such time-efficient assessments as "notebook surrogates," in which students describe a scientific investigation so clearly and logically that a friend can then repeat the same steps accurately. Shavelson and Baxter contend that such methods are inexpensive and fairly easy to assess—about one to two minutes per student. If these notebooks are rubric scored, we will have progressive, numerical data to mark improvement and use as a base for instructional adjustments throughout the school year.

More elaborate assessments can occur regularly but less frequently. Sizer (1992) provides a good example of the kind of science assessment that can be periodically administered to determine how well students' scientific knowledge is transferring to more lifelike contexts. Students are asked to act as nutritionists to design and defend three menus. Each menu must meet the following criteria:

- Stay within a budget of $2.56 per serving.
- Meet the requirements for maximum nutrition.
- Be attractive to students.

Even occasional assessments such as these supplement—and
inform—the traditional science curriculum, which all the science
foundations are unanimous in telling us are too long on content and
short on application.

Bill Walther, a science teacher at La Cima Middle School in our
district, uses a portfolio system. It contains items like an "Acid Rain
Journal," which reveals students' ability to use "data to support
conclusions and generalizations." His rubrics consist of clear, descriptive criteria to assess four levels of achievement:

E: Exceptional Work
Q: Quality Work
I: In Progress
N: Needs Rethinking or Completion

Accompanying each rubric are descriptors that focus on a quality
product and evidence that students are developing a scientific dispo-
sition—that their work "shows evidence of a solid understanding of
the assignment or task" and that they demonstrate the ability to
"provide alternative approaches to solving problems."

In the Pomperaug Regional School District, students are assigned
designated tasks at the primary, elementary, and upper elementary
levels. At each level, they must complete tasks from four major
categories: (1) "Scientific Process," (2) "Graphs and Related Products,"
(3) "Science Products," and (4) "Communication Products Using
Science Content." Each category has 6 to 10 common performance
tasks for students to complete; each task has assessments and criteria.

Most schools are not this organized. But teachers at any grade or
level can get started by selecting areas of strong emphasis or agreement
in the science curriculum, developing one or more assessment tasks
for those areas, and building from there. One simple approach is to
modify an activity that most teachers already do. Eventually, common
tasks and assessments—even content mastery tests—can be developed
for each quarter or semester and the results gathered and analyzed.

Such an effort can begin with one common test or performance
task evaluated with the same criteria. Teachers can then compile the
collective results anonymously to see how their own students compare to the group standard. This comparison immediately creates the
opportunity to examine the most exemplary student work and hence
to move toward uniformly interpreting the assessment criteria. Once
teachers feel comfortable with the first step, they can select another
task or a comprehensive or end-of-term assessment. Teachers have
autonomy while they move carefully toward a reasonable level of
consensus on what they want students to learn about science. As such
efforts begin to pull teachers and their collective brainpower together,
the benefits for students will be enormous.

88   Frequent, Collective Assessment—Not as Daunting as It Seems

Regular, collective assessment isn't as difficult as it may at first seem. It is as easy as (1) getting a team of teachers together to review year-end state or district summative tests, or the skills the teachers will measure that year, and (2) selecting or developing a small but representative handful of problems to develop short-term assessments and subgoals. One each quarter—or even each semester—can get the process started.

That's what Dan Hendery and his math team at Johnson City High School did. And they got remarkable results. They created a battery of assessments by reviewing past copies of the New York Regents exam. They quickly selected about 25 representative problems for each exam and administered them quarterly. After each assessment, they conducted an item analysis—together—in which they discussed problems or areas where students were notably strong or struggling. The result? The first year, the percentage of students succeeding on the Regents exam rose from 47 to 93 percent. They now use this approach to promote success in math at the elementary level as well. Such a simple, quarterly strategy allows both teachers and students to head off failure before the end of the year, when it is too late to help. These exams have been easy to use and update yearly. Teachers can swap problems as the summative exams evolve or add multistep problems and alternative assessments as emphases shift.

A team from one of our schools, Holaway Elementary, realized continuous improvement as members gathered data using a 3-part rubric they created for math. Part 1 measured student performance in computation; Part 2, logical reasoning (as seen through student writing); and Part 3, demonstration (skillful and appropriate use of equations). At regularly scheduled meetings lasting about 30 minutes, they analyzed the data on just one multistep problem (a great way for any team to get started) to see what was working and which areas most needed shoring up. Then they brainstormed for solutions to problems the data revealed. In each of the three areas, they saw steady improvement; Figure 7.4 shows how students improved in logical reasoning.

Improvement like this is doable. We don't need to wait until a full-blown battery of assessments is firmly established in every state or district—which themselves are always subject to change (as it should be). We must begin where we are and move forward immediately by starting small and capitalizing on what's at hand.

Connecticut's Pomperaug Regional School District has developed one of the most sophisticated and impressive alternative assessment programs in the United States. Even so, administrators urge teachers to start small as they move into the world of performance assessment, to select a project that they "already assign to their students," and to "make this task a short, simple, and easy one." Assistant Superintendent Michael Hibbard recommends starting with a team or department that is willing to experiment with one performance assessment. The aim is to promote immediate but ongoing, incremental improvement.

FIGURE 7.4

Percentage of Students Achieving Level 3 or Higher on Logical Reasoning, One of Three Areas Measured in a Math Rubric*

1994–95 School Year

*The 4-point rubric measures performance in computation, logical reasoning, and demonstration.
Source: Holaway Elementary School, Tucson, Arizona.

Ted Sizer's book, *Horace's School: Redesigning the American High School* (1992), is punctuated with suggested exhibitions that can serve as excellent benchmark assessments for data-driven, throughout-the-year improvements. For example, one exhibition asks students to decide whether they should buy a 1988 Ford Tempo or a 1988 Toyota Corolla. They are required to address the following concerns:

90

- Mileage
- Price of the car and cost of insurance
- Impact of the cost over four years relative to earnings
- Impact relative to entertainment budget

Such problems and assessments can easily be matched or tailored for quarterly or end-of-unit assessments. Teams of teachers offering the same course can set these types of subgoals at department meetings or special sessions, then analyze the results.

Let's look at how some of the better report cards can provide opportunities for data-based improvement. As we've seen, opportunities for data-based improvement in report cards are springing up in school districts throughout the United States. For example, on its report cards, the Kyrene School District lists indicators to monitor student success in math:

- Counts to 50/100/Beyond 100.
- Skip-counts by 10's/5's/2's.
- Uses strategies to solve problem situations.
- Makes and reads simple graphs.

Teachers can monitor aggregate data on grade-level and school-wide student success in these areas, either in a general collaboration or a more data-driven scheme. Analyzing data and developing strategies on how to promote collective progress (e.g., the number or percentage of students who are mastering each task and the best ways to improve that number) reveal opportunities to achieve short-term, breakthrough results. These results can be prominently charted, showing the incremental impact of faculty collaboration and adjustment to instruction as teachers strive to help greater numbers of students.

Knowing Where They Stand

In any subject area, students and teachers want to know where they stand in relation to achievable standards. When we work to improve—at anything—knowing how well we're doing is essential. An increasing amount of evidence indicates that providing this information helps students. As we have seen, Colorado's Weld County School District has had great success by carefully monitoring both individual and aggregate student progress in writing, reading, and math, using a continuous improvement, TQM model. Teachers take great pains to ensure that all students have truly reached requisite levels of achievement before moving on—a fairly radical departure from what happens in the average school (Waters, Burger, and Burger 1995).

Results Among the Disciplines   91

Some results span the disciplines. The first three discussed here are gaining momentum: the ability to make oral presentations, to participate effectively in discussions, and to read critically and interpretively. They may seem to have their home in the language arts. But they are increasingly being seen as important elements of a quality education in every subject area.

The Oral Presentation

Like writing, making effective presentations has implications for every discipline. The ability to orally present, propose, and persuade is a key skill and can provide intrinsic motivation for students to find purpose in their studies. Learning, without any opportunities to share what we've learned, is a little like cooking for ourselves; we do it, but we probably won't do it as well. One of the most exciting and energized classrooms I have ever seen was a high school business and careers class taught by Dolores Christensen at Gilbert High School in Gilbert, Arizona. I was amazed to learn that only students who were two or more years behind in their core courses were eligible for the course. When I asked Dolores what the secret for such enthusiastic activity was, she said, without hesitating, that the weekly oral presentations the students had to do lent immediacy and purpose to their research.

The Key School in downtown Indianapolis had the prescience to make the oral presentation the cornerstone of their assessment program. A videotape of several student presentations per year follows students throughout their school career.

Baltimore's Walbrook High School, a member of the Coalition of Essential Schools, has made the oral presentation a key exhibition for students to demonstrate mastery for high school graduation.

Here at Amphitheater High School, a team of English and social studies teachers developed a rubric to evaluate student oral presentations. Part of the rubric evaluated students' introductions to their presentations, using the following criteria:

- Arouses interest.
- Is appropriate to the topic.
- Is brief and to the point.

Though the main goal is to measurably improve the quality of oral presentations, an excellent subgoal that teachers pursued for a period was better introductions (which their data revealed was an area where students seemed to have the most difficulty). This subgoal approach resulted in a continuously higher percentage of students

92   making quality oral presentations "at or above standard" during the 1994-95 school year: from 32 percent in October, to 58 percent in December, to 64 percent in March.

Our district is preparing to pilot the oral presentation for all levels. Included are the following criteria, which serve as subgoals to pursue incremental, continuous improvement:

- Use of visual aids.
- Evidence of organization.
- Logical defense of a position.

Walbrook High School in Baltimore used this same focused, analytical approach to achieve documented improvement in the quality of student presentations. Notice how improvement in any of the following areas can constitute a subgoal. But notice as well how rich yet common-sensical they are. By collaboratively viewing and discussing student presentations, Walbrook teachers decided to take the following improvement actions:

- Schedule oral presentations earlier in the year.
- Do more to suggest topics to students within areas of interest.
- Ask students to do a trial run and refine it during their junior year for their senior year presentation.
- Make the criteria for evaluation more specific (Turner and Finney 1993).

The team at Amphitheater High School came up with the following suggestions after one collaborative session:

- Hand out rubrics in advance of all assignments.
- Show and analyze the best model presentations on videotape.
- Make sure students practice more frequently but for smaller groups rather than for the entire class.
- Help students concentrate on and rehearse introductions, an area of major difficulty.

The insights contained in the preceding lists show that collaboration allows teachers to capture each other's fund of collective intelligence. A clear goal optimizes the quality of their sharing; they are organized to succeed. In the isolation and crush of events that is a teacher's life, time to evaluate and refocus is limited. The list from Amphitheater High School is from a longer list of 23 suggestions for improvement generated by the team—in 15 minutes. Some of the teachers said that they learned more from each other in that 15 minutes than at any other time. Their effort paid off, for them and

for the students, who expressed a high level of satisfaction at having
the opportunity to sharpen their speaking skills.

Improving Discussion Skills

Let's look at another related area for results—discussion. Documents such as the U.S. Department of Labor's SCANS report (Secretary's Commission on Achieving Necessary Skills 1992) tell us that the ability to speak, listen, and interact intelligently is emerging as one of the pivotal proficiencies in the workplace of the future. Other research supports this conclusion:

> In the economy of the 21st century, all indications are that
> speaking and listening will be among the most important skills
> (Daggett 1994, pp. 20–21).

Substantive discussions are also among the best settings to exercise and enlarge one's intellectual and reasoning capacities:

> Discussion is the most basic and essential form of participatory
> citizenship. It is in discussion that disagreements are revealed,
> clarified, and analyzed; alternatives created and explored...
> common purposes perceived; decisions made; action planned.
> Talk is not cheap (Parker 1991, p. vi).

Unfortunately, discussion has been relegated to the periphery of skills and activities that make up the school day. Nonetheless, the Coalition of Essential Schools, as well as the Paideia Program, have seen it as being at the very heart of an education. The Paideia Program goes so far as to recommend that about a third of a student's school time be spent examining and analyzing ideas in discussion (Adler 1982). Research conducted in Amphitheater reveals that students count discussion among their favorite and most stimulating school activities. (The Junior Great Books Foundation provides excellent training in conducting guided discussions.)

Peter Cookson's (1985) study of the best private schools in the United States shows more profound implications. It reveals that regular participation in discussions is one of the most distinguishing features of these institutions. The recurring opportunity to articulate and interpret ideas gives their graduates a decided advantage in making their way in the world.

Most school discussions are restricted to recall, parroting material just read. According to Gamoran and Nystrand (1992), an average student's school week includes *little or no discussion* that invites students to interpret and express ideas and opinions. This is regret-

94

table. We should begin to see dialogue as one of the most engaging, intellectually enlarging activities we have for promoting the listening and critical thinking skills that students need so badly. It is at the heart of democratic participation, equipping a citizenry for the responsibility of self-government.

Discussion is a skill we should assess, especially in the early grades, when some students are likely to get left behind their more assertive classmates. Assessment helps ensure that all students have the opportunity to acquire a facility with discussion. Stiggins (1994) describes a process that he calls "scored discussions"; students can produce criteria such as the following to evaluate the discussions:

- Listening attentively when others are contributing.
- Asking clarifying questions.
- Making points clear and brief.
- Being confident to take a position and defend it.

Such criteria can serve as subgoals and be developed into a discussion rubric. One way to assess a discussion is for students to assemble themselves into two circles, one inside the other. The group in the inner circle discusses, while the group on the periphery documents and tallies data on the frequency and quality of the contributions that the inside group makes. Subgoals can include trying to reach an ever-higher number of students, quarterly or monthly, who are improving in a specific subskill (e.g., making points clear and brief) or who can perform at or above standard (e.g., satisfying the criteria or earning a "3" or "4" on a 4-point discussion rubric).

Reading

Reading is another area that spans the disciplines. In the lower grades, reading means acquiring the basic skills of decoding and comprehension. After students learn the basics of construing text, they need to learn the art of mining a text for meaning. As my friend Wayne Dotts likes to say, they pass from "learning to read" to "reading to learn."

Learning to Read. Rapid advances are occurring in our ability to teach reading, especially in our ability to monitor progress and adjust teaching practice. The success of programs such as Reading Recovery, Success for All, and Reading Renaissance is built on the notion we have been stressing:

> Successful early-intervention programs include systematic regular assessment in order to monitor progress and provide a basis for instructional planning (Pikulski 1994, p. 37).

The Success for All program has succeeded in almost every school where it has been used (Slavin et al. 1994). One cornerstone practice is giving quarterly tests, which provide information for the express purpose of informing and adjusting instruction to get better results.

In addition to giving tests for improving results, another ongoing goal (or subgoal) can be to increase the number of lower-achieving students who graduate out of the remedial pullout component in the programs, by reaching reading levels where they no longer need individual tutoring sessions to keep up with their peers.

Many successful intervention programs include similar indicators, which teachers use to gauge student progress:

- Ability to recognize prescribed sight words.
- Ability to identify all lowercase and uppercase letters.
- Ability to recognize phonemic cues and consonant blends.

These, too, are emerging on report cards, providing focus for teachers and richer information for parents, thus creating clear goals for all to work toward. The 1st grade report card for the Ann Arbor Public Schools includes the following indicators:

- Reads fluently at his or her reading level.
- Demonstrates knowledge of story structure.
- Identifies the topic and two or more supporting details of an informational book read to students.

Teachers can monitor the pace at which groups of children work, from "not yet" to "developing," to "achieving" in these areas. The data can be used to identify areas of primary concern from quarter to quarter and help teachers reach year-end reading proficiency goals.

Reading to Learn. The potential for student benefit is enormous in this area. Consider the manifold applications of the goal shown in Figure 7.5, adapted from a state-level reading rubric. The goal merges reading and writing: Students write to reveal their skill as thoughtful, perceptive readers. Again, as helpful as such criteria may be for focusing and identifying short-term subgoals, there is no substitute for models and anchor papers that reveal student ability to express sound interpretation in writing. Abundant opportunities exist within and among every discipline for students to produce written evidence of careful, perceptive reading. Offering students the opportunity to examine exemplary pieces not only adds flesh to the descriptions and criteria but also provides a nonthreatening guide and guards against gross variations in standards.

FIGURE 7.5
Goal and Subgoals for Reading

Goal: All students can demonstrate a complex understanding and interpretation of a text.
   Subgoals: All students will demonstrate
   • Considerable evidence of extension of the text (connection to other texts, experiences, and generalizations).
   • Evidence of "reading like a writer": evaluating and appreciating author's perspectives and craft.
   • Ability to address all elements of a higher-order interpretive question about a text.

Source: Adapted from a reading rubric in the Arizona State Assessment Program, Arizona Department of Education, Phoenix.

The Research Paper

Amphitheater schools have developed a set of benchmark assessments and standards within and among the subject areas. These will measure authentic student achievement at five different benchmark points along the K–12 continuum. At each benchmark, criteria have been carefully established and refined by teams of teachers.

The first assessment we are piloting districtwide is the Research Paper Project, which our teachers are using either within a subject area or as part of an interdisciplinary effort. Withal, virtually every student in the district now completes a research paper that requires them not only to record but to critically process information. We now have baseline data from the 1994–95 school year. These will provide our baseline for districtwide improvements in the next few years.

But several schools are already doing *periodic* assessments during the 1994–95 school year to promote short-term continuous improvement. At Nash Elementary, students are writing a research paper each quarter. At the end of the first quarter, teachers collected and graphed schoolwide data on how well students were doing relative to the district criteria, which includes Content, Process, Critical Thinking, Style, and Mechanics. Using these data, they have identified students' major areas of difficulty, which then informs their action planning. Nash's "breakthrough" goal for this year is for each student to demonstrate improvement in at least two areas *each quarter*. This strategy should promote considerable improvement by the end of the school year. Interestingly, while emphasizing the research paper,

Nash realized a simultaneous and significant improvement in stand-ardized test scores.

Student Responsibility and Behavior

Student responsibility and behavior are an integral part of growth and development; they dramatically affect the academic climate of a school (Blase 1986, McPherson 1972, Lickona 1991).

James Fitzpatrick is a former principal and superintendent. While he was principal at Champlain Valley High School in Burlington, Vermont, he instituted a set of innovative disciplinary practices. He believed that the burden for order and responsibility should be on students, including giving them more of a part in determining the rules they would live by and the consequences of their misbehavior. In the first year he implemented his system, the cost for repairs from vandalism dropped from $12,000 to $1,200. Suspensions were re-duced from 90 to 9. For the six following years, the school did not have to suspend any children. Because the intent of this new ap-proach was to re-engage, rather than to punish students, the dropout rate fell from about 7.5 percent to between 0.5 percent and 2.7 percent annually *over the next seven years*. The new system dealt so effectively with students in a conventional school setting that one of the two alternative schools was closed.

At one of our schools, Keeling Elementary, the number of violent incidents during one school year was reduced from 99 to 4 when the school implemented a new policy on campus fights. The school had no doubts about the policy's effectiveness.

La Cima Middle School instituted a new responsibility plan that produced significant results. From June 1992 to June 1994, the number of incidents in the category of "campus/classroom disrup-tions" was reduced from 588 to 402. The number of unexcused absences and tardies, as well as incidents of vandalism, theft, and arson, was halved.

As many schools are demonstrating, the concept of responsibility can embrace a larger set of behaviors. Figure 7.6 shows part of a 4-point responsibility rubric used at Nash Elementary School in our district. The rubric also includes descriptions of nondisruptive behav-ior (not included in the figure). Data on students, class, and school performance on this rubric are collected and charted regularly—even weekly in some classes. A 2nd grade teacher at Nash pointed out how effective it is for him to chart his class's behavioral performance daily and weekly. He likes to say things such as, "Look at this. We had a great day yesterday. Most of us are at '4'—what are we going to do today? Let's do it again."

FIGURE 7.6
Level 4 Criteria for a 4-Point Rubric for Responsibility

- Student demonstrates self-regulation by setting and following through on goals and by regularly monitoring and reflecting on behavior.
- Student is resourceful and knows how to seek assistance when necessary.
- Student is dependable and meets obligations and deadlines.

Source: Nash Elementary School, Tucson, Arizona.

Such imaginative use of a responsibility rubric has had measurable dividends for the teacher and the school. It creates clear, understandable goals and subgoals for students and staff.

"Unconventional" and Affective Measures

Throughout this book, I have stressed the primary importance of academic goals and lamented the perennial avoidance of striving for clear learning and behavior targets that we can measure progress toward. We are wise to remember what Joyce, Wolf, and Calhoun (1993) tell us: They "did not find a single case in the literature where student learning increased but had not been a central goal" (p. 19).

Academic goals, however, do not preclude using other kinds of goals and measures. We can expand the idea of results to include measures of processes that are a step or two removed from actual student achievement or behavior. When coupled with a vigilant attendance to achievement or behavior, such measures can bring about positive change.

"Unconventional measures," a term Peters (1987, pp. 491–492) uses, can be among the most significant and effective ways to foster change where it counts. Speaking in the context of business, he advocates that we embrace and elevate the status of some commonplace activities by gauging and displaying the number or percentage of each:

- People or teams involved in "small starts" (improvement efforts).
- Rewards given for quality.
- Pilot projects.
- Ideas swiped from competitors.
- People working in teams.
- Recognition acts or events per month.

- Time spent per day or week on a top priority.
- Hours and dollars devoted to upgrading skills.

Many of these activities will translate to school settings. Similarly, schools may measure and chart progress toward other goals:

- Training (e.g., the number of teachers confidently employing more engaging, interactive, and constructivist learning techniques).
- Number of team-based improvement efforts.
- Number of goal and data-driven improvement efforts.
- Number of good ideas disseminated and adapted.

Or what about measures that help us adjust processes to move toward the goal of increasing the number of students who complete assignments? The root causes for why students don't turn work in—not just homework but all assignments—may reveal ways we can incrementally enhance the quality and capacity of school work to arrest their energies. The 9th grade "Freshman Forum" program at Amphitheater's Canyon Del Oro High School found a strong correlation between student failure and failure to turn work in. On the basis of this information, the Forum teachers brainstormed for strategies to help ensure that more students would complete and turn in assignments. The results of their preliminary efforts were at least modestly encouraging.

The issue of work completed brings us to a cornerstone issue—and another ripe opportunity. Both Goodlad in the 1970s and Lounsbury and Clark as recently as 1990 have given us the grim news: For a vast majority of students, school is too often a series of passive and often boring activities. Haberman (1990) tells us that the most disadvantaged and disaffected students are being fed a diet of meaningless drill and worksheets, even though such methods were "never proven by research or practice." Numerous studies, including those by Newmann (1992), and by Means, Chelemer, and Knapp (1991), point out what common sense should have already told us: Students don't learn much from dull, meaningless exercises and assignments. This situation may be one of the root causes for student disaffection, especially in secondary school where it is most pronounced.

One way to measure progress in this area is to document how schools are becoming more challenging, enjoyable, and engaging places to learn. At Hollibrook Elementary School, teachers ask students directly about their level of satisfaction with their experience there. As many as 90 percent have indicated that they enjoy school and like their teachers.

100   A consortium of schools called the North Carolina Project have attempted to invigorate science instruction by introducing a more active, hands-on curriculum. Part of what the schools wanted to accomplish in the short term was a new attitude toward science. They succeeded—in spades. After only one year of implementation, the percentage of consortium students reporting that they like science rose from 38 to 87 percent (O'Neil 1992).

Social Behavior and Character Development

One category on the 1st grade report card in the Ann Arbor Public Schools is "Learning and Social Behaviors." Included with the academic indicators are items that measure behavior:

- Demonstrates self-control.
- Follows directions.
- Completes tasks independently.
- Respects the rights of others.

In any school, the data in such areas can provide a rewarding context for collaboration. For example, if the data indicated a persistent problem in following directions, teachers can discuss democratic procedures that heighten student buy-in and understanding of classroom rules. The data would regularly reveal progress and areas most needing intervention.

One of the most creatively data-driven school districts I have visited is the Clovis, California, schools, which have an exceptionally strong tradition of promoting measurable growth in the areas of "Mind, Body, and Spirit." The Clovis schools developed imaginative ways to promote and measure "Spirit" and character development long before such activity was fashionable. Teachers systematically gather data on student involvement in volunteer activities, which they believe are tantamount to character development. At some schools, students acquire points for a variety of activities:

- Maintaining a flower bed on campus.
- Helping clean up after a dance.
- Visiting a nursing home.
- Participating in extracurricular activities (which in our district correlates closely with students staying in school).

Students accumulate points to work toward the goal of earning enough to receive an award recognizing their accomplishment. Principal Richard Sparks of Valley Oak Elementary School in Clovis spoke enthusiastically about the increasing number of students who have earned the "Exemplary Wildcat Award" over the years. These results are discussed regularly, as teachers develop new strategies for reaching out to more and more kids who benefit from the experiences these programs offer. These, too, are meaningful results.

The Challenge

The challenge, especially in the beginning, is to be supremely protective of the number of goals we pursue formally—the goals for which we establish regular times for analyzing data and planning for improvement. These other goals, though important, do not—should not—supplant the central academic goals of a school. They are meaningful subgoals and ancillary goals, but the frequent and regular time and attention needed to reach learning and behavioral goals must take precedence. As we have seen so many times, schools can make progress toward affective and procedural goals and still not make any substantive progress in student learning. This tension is resolved by being ever watchful of the results that represent a school's primary academic and behavioral mission.

Taking Advantage of Available Data

Even before we have the chance to develop and refine more sophisticated assessments and ways of measuring progress, we would be smart to capitalize on the many opportunities we have to begin gathering meaningful data immediately. We in Amphitheater are learning from the Frederick County Public Schools, where school improvement teams set goals and then make use of whatever data are appropriate—and available. Steve Hess, their director of assessment, shared how this approach can include the most available and easily assembled data:

- Number or percentage of students on the honor roll by quarter.
- Number or percentage of students receiving an *A* or *B* in subject areas that are the focus of the year's goals.
- Decrease in number or percentage of students receiving *D* or *F* in specified subjects.
- Number of students completing algebra or geometry.
- Reduction in the number of students moving out of the lowest quartile.
- Schoolwide GPA.

Again, no single measure ever fully or perfectly captures the fullness of our achievements or capacities. But measurement can be an important part of our attempt to excel, to improve in an informed and confident manner toward our goals.

Bank the Best

It can take an exceedingly long time to acquire first-rate assessments for all the areas mentioned in this chapter. Therefore, we must bank, borrow, share, and organize the best assessments to make them available to every teacher in our schools, states, and districts. Pomperaug and Frederick County schools, as well as the Maryland State Assessment Consortium, have made a science of pooling their best assessments. Their teachers can choose from a wealth of fine assessments and evaluation criteria that are refined yearly. Frederick County teachers believe they saved years by working to develop high-quality assessments with 16 other districts. These assessments can be purchased and adapted by any interested district.

So what are we waiting for? From the conventional to the more sophisticated, we have opportunities in every area to begin gauging—and getting—improved results.

Conclusion: Leadership

If I had enough ribbon, I could conquer the world.

—Napoleon Bonaparte

Change throughout the system will not come about through a thousand points of light, but from the steadily increasing, concentrated light and heat of one sun.

—Donahoe 1993

Celebrate, Recognize, Reinforce, and Reward

The kind of significant, sustained improvement that we need in schools will not occur in an isolated, free-lance culture, where no one knows what anyone else is doing or what each other's operative goals are. That is a system in disarray.

Schools improve when purpose and effort unite. One key is leadership that recognizes its most vital function: to keep everyone's eyes on the prize of improved student learning. The crush of competing agendas and distractions does not make that focus easy.

One of the most effective means to cultivate a goal-oriented culture is to regularly reinforce and recognize improvement efforts, both privately and publicly. The business world is beginning to realize the importance of such recognition, which brings an organization closer to its goals (Peters 1987). But not schools. Lortie (1975) found that schools were conspicuously lacking a sense of pride or achievement, that individual as well as group recognition of progress or success was extremely rare. More recent research by Evans (1993) indicates that "in most schools, recognition levels are chronically low," at a time when the challenges of change make such recognition and reinforcement more important than ever (p. 22).

We are failing to take advantage of what students in both business and industry tell us may be the most potent and effective aspect of leadership, with the best chance of promoting change and

104   improvement (Peters 1987, Blase and Kirby 1992). Little (1987) asserts
           that for teachers to work effectively together, "the accomplishments
           of individuals and groups must be recognized and celebrated" (p.
           514). Sincere, regular praise, plus recognition and celebration of
           accomplishment, may be the most overlooked ingredient in results-
           oriented leadership. Blase and Kirby (1992) found that praise from
           administration was the most frequently cited source of good feelings,
           and that most teachers have unfulfilled needs for recognition and
           approval. Lortie's (1975) observations indicate that this need has a
           direct impact on a school's ability to get results:

> [The] modesty of occasions which produce prideful feelings
> underscores the difficulty teachers see in attaining worthwhile
> results (p. 133).

He found that teachers "crave reassurance which, for them, could
only come from superordinates or teaching peers." The absence of
this reassurance not only "reduces the joy" of teaching but also leads
many teachers to seek professional fulfillment by concentrating only
on their strong suits—and giving short shrift to subject areas or
students who make them feel less successful (Lortie 1975, p. 141).

Teachers can guide themselves in many meaningful ways, but
principals and other leaders have a responsibility to reinforce individual and collective effort. The school community can help by
taking the time to establish common goals that direct not just
individuals but all faculty members in a socially interactive, mutually
reinforcing effort. Establishing goals is a manifestation of leadership,
but it is only the beginning in a results-oriented framework. Just as
regular consultation of data and indicators is essential to sustained,
targeted effort, so also is regular praise, recognition, and celebration
necessary to keep the effort focused and energized. Success and
improvement are every bit as social as they are structural. An atmosphere of acknowledgment and appreciation is essential.

Administrators at every level can be more effective if they use
concrete strategies to celebrate and recognize goal-oriented effort and
achievement. Praise and public acknowledgment that "yes, you or
your team really do make a difference" is both confirming and
affirming in a culture that has traditionally been marked by a high
level of "uncertainty" about the significance of its contributions
(Lortie 1975, pp. 134–136). Attempts to more regularly and publicly
appreciate quality efforts can make a difference—more than perhaps
any other factor (Blase and Kirby 1992, Peters 1987).

Goals, Data, and Leadership: A Reciprocal Relationship   105

Again, the first step is to establish goals. Goals and data make achievement clear and intelligible, hence easier for a busy leader to recognize. In Frederick County, Maryland, schools have given year-end dinners for members of school improvement teams to publicly celebrate the goals achieved at each site. In Amphitheater schools, Superintendent Richard Wilson has asked teams of teachers to give presentations to school and district administrators, describing their data-driven success in reaching their goals. Efforts like these provide a public forum for praise, while providing explicit and inspiring examples of what an organization most values.

Initial improvement efforts are not always sustained. We have seen how improvement ceases when a gifted leader moves on. Leadership should lead to results; if we wish to see a new generation of leaders who can truly lead us to better results, then we must adjust the system to facilitate such leadership.

The new culture of schools should encourage and expect that a leader will orchestrate a program that includes measurable goals, as well as regular praise and celebration of progress toward those goals. "Leadership" should "demand short-term results" and thus "spread hope" (Chang, Labovitz, and Rosansky 1992, pp. 101–102). Our graduate schools and leadership academies should teach such leadership. Without a set of common goals, schools will not be able to sustain their efforts, hope will dwindle, and low expectations may set in. With it, the entire school community can work as one. Collaboration will not happen, however, if goals are too numerous, superficial, or unmeasurable.

Leadership must unite. In her studies, Little (1990) remarks on the gross, unsettling inconsistency in activities and emphases she observed among teachers all supposedly teaching the same subject—English. Managing a "thousand points of light" is feckless and probably impossible. But we don't have to advocate a rigid, lockstep uniformity for leaders to effectively manage a coherent, unified effort to help more kids learn to write, read, and use mathematical knowledge.

Celebration, recognition, and reward only require a varied repertoire of methods and a sincere heart. Teachers must believe that the methods are more than a bald attempt to manipulate or control behavior. They must see praise and recognition as an extension of a leader's character (Blase and Kirby 1992).

Praise must also be tied to specific successes, even targeted to both individual and group accomplishments. The result, as teachers them-

106   selves attest, is a more focused, creative, positive, and supportive faculty. To bring about this result, leaders can use some of the following methods:

- Leaving notes in boxes or on a desk, complimenting effective instruction that was observed.
- Giving coffee mugs for individual or group achievements.
- Offering a trinket or gift (a big favorite in one workplace was candy bars).
- Briefly, but frequently, praising, celebrating, and recognizing efforts at faculty meetings or board meetings.
- Prominently featuring graphs and charts—similar to the United Way thermometer—where employees can regularly view their progress and school leaders can easily refer to goal-oriented progress.
- Providing opportunities for successful teams to share their accomplishments in brief presentations at administrative meetings. Perhaps every major meeting should begin with such presentations.
- Providing opportunities for individuals to share a goal-oriented success with other groups or school faculties.
- Ensuring that every issue of the school or district newsletter highlights team and individual accomplishments; some whole issues could contain banner headlines, some with charts and graphs revealing growth.

"Field" of Dreams, Where Progress and Recognition Prevail

Many teachers work in near anonymity, regardless of their daily and weekly accomplishments. They deserve recognition; our schools can only benefit from granting it. When deserving people are not appropriately appreciated for all they do, entropy may rush in. In her book, *Leadership and the New Science*, Margaret Wheatley (1994) likens organizational life to what physicists call a field, which consists of particles. Fields—bad or good—form as "particles" converge to create a palpable reality. "Vision," morale, and the spirit of an organization are a function of the particles that create a field—prevailing and evolving thoughts and conversations that occur in thousands of situations (pp. 47–56). Amphitheater schools Superintendent Richard Wilson points out the importance of "ongoing dialogue and reminders. When you talk about results, you sharpen your focus. This talk in itself promotes a sharpening of focus and a sure sense of purpose."

Unfortunately, the spirit of many organizations, regardless of their written vision statements or beliefs, reveals a lack of critical density. Into this vacuum can rush rumor, mistrust, and negativism.

The organization becomes aimless—a mass of "contradicting
fields...a jumble of behaviors," with no clear purpose (Wheatley
1994, pp. 56–57).

Leaders, then, must be what Wheatley calls broadcasters, target-
ing praise and recognition to create a unified, purposeful culture or
field. Developing a positive, productive, and fulfilling field in a
school or district means providing contexts and flashpoints that
promote positive and productive thoughts and conversations. If we
frequently clarify and celebrate progress toward goals and the impact
of our efforts on students, we help to sustain the conditions essential
to a healthy, ever-improving workplace. Just as important are efforts
to recognize, reward, and celebrate accomplishments, which work
pre-emptively to ward off the destructive thoughts and conversations
that are the inevitable result when an organization ignores the social
and psychological needs of its people.

Leaders must facilitate this. They must bring the field into
being—and broadcast confidence in what the organization can
achieve. Thoreau tells us to advance confidently toward our dreams,
even to build "castles in the air....That is where they should be. Now
put the foundations under them" (Thoreau 1946, p. 21). Management theorist Russel Ackoff (1978) encourages leaders to lead participants in a discussion of the perfect organization and the loftiest
goals—to construct an "idealized redesign" based on their loftiest
aspirations (p. 189). Then the group can brainstorm for practical ways
to realize the dream. He describes his concept:

> An idealized redesign of a system reveals that the principal
> obstructions between an organization and what it most wants
> to be lie within the organization, and that these barriers can
> be removed (p. 190).

Leaders are uniquely positioned to ensure that amid the busyness
and bombardment that all organizations endure, the dream remains
central. Leaders nourish the dream by keeping each person fully
aware of an organization's purpose and goals. Individuals also need
to know that, without a doubt, their efforts contribute meaningfully
to the purpose and goals. By providing brief but regular occasions to
observe, recognize, celebrate, and reward meaningful accomplishments, leaders can create a field of dreams where progress and
appreciation prevail.

Collective Brainpower—The Key to Results

This book attempts to influence the field that is our current
school culture—in both what it does and how it thinks. The thoughts

108   expressed here are offered with the confidence that the teachers, schools, and scholars mentioned in these pages demonstrate the power of these enduring principles. They rescue us from mere "reforms," from "initiatives," to issue in what Glickman calls "solid, enduring results" for our children. Together, these principles point up the importance of taking full and systematic advantage of the greatest yet most underestimated resource we have at our disposal in the service of results: individual and collective intelligence. When we harness and organize this intelligence, improvement occurs. But if we want the stuff of dreams—sustained improvement on a wide, even national scale—only leadership will get us there. This work should not be the sole responsibility of leaders, however, who work in a difficult climate, trying to establish priorities, measure progress, and address a school's central goals. All of us, from community members to teachers to administrators, have a tremendous influence on this climate. We are all in a position to influence the field on which the battle for better schools is taking place.

Appendix:
Effective,
Time-Efficient
Meetings

The following model enables a team to have a productive meeting in about 30 minutes (which is often all that is available).[1] It can be tailored to fit a group's specific purposes. The approximate number of minutes for each part is in parentheses.

Before the Meeting

- **Agenda.** Was the agenda distributed in advance of the meeting? Is it posted in clear view of the participants?
- **Recording Tools.** Is flip chart, chalkboard, or computer ready to record brainstorming?
- **Designated Tasks.** Have the timekeeper, recorder, and facilitator been appointed?

During the Meeting

The team leader should establish and articulate the purpose of the meeting: What outcomes are desired? (The general purpose proposed for these meetings is to identify major concerns and strategies to promote better results for an agreed-upon goal.)*(1 minute)*

---

[1]The model was designed by Rosemary Beck, Bill Bendt, and Chris Potter, teachers in the Amphitheater School District, Tucson, Arizona.

110

Strategies That Worked *(5 minutes)*

What worked? The team leader gives each member a chance to offer evidence of a strategy that was effective in helping reach the goal since the last meeting.[2]

Chief Challenges *(3–5 minutes)*

What is the most urgent concern, problem, or obstacle to progress and better results?

Proposed Solutions *(8–10 minutes)*

What are possible concrete, practical solutions to these problems?

Action Plan *(10 minutes)*

- Which solutions might be best for the team to focus on between now and the next meeting? For example, if the goal or subgoal is "to increase the number of quality introductions," the team might focus on a strategy such as, "students will analyze model introductions before attempting to revise their own." (If agreement does not emerge quickly, rank-order voting to determine the focus may be useful).

- If appropriate, the team may need to determine and record the names of the people who are responsible for specific tasks prior to the next meeting.

After the Meeting

The team leader distributes a memo documenting the team's focus between now and the next meeting. (A memo may not be necessary if brainstorming is done on a computer or using an LCD [liquid crystal display]; memos can then be printed out and distributed almost immediately.)

Summary

The meetings enable every team member to quickly and efficiently take advantage of the maximum number of concrete ideas and each member's acquired expertise on a clear goal and strategic focus.

---

[2]The emphasis should be on *concision*. You may want to limit the time for each brainstorming contribution by applying what Allied Signal Corporation calls the "20-second rule." This method not only increases the amount of ideas that each member generates but also heightens energy level, focus, and clarity of expression.

References

Ackerman, D.B. (1989). "Intellectual and Practical Criteria for Successful Curriculum Integration." In *Interdisciplinary Curriculum: Design and Implementation*, edited by H.H. Jacobs. Alexandria, Va.: Association for Supervision and Curriculum Development.

Ackoff, R. (1978). *The Art of Problem Solving*. New York: Wiley.

Adler, M. (1982). *The Paideia Proposal*. New York: Collier.

Andrade, J., and H. Ryley. (November 1992). "A Quality Approach to Writing Assessment." *Educational Leadership* 50, 3: 22–23.

Arizona Daily Star. (July 21, 1994). "Inner City School Pesters, Prods Pupils onto College," p. A1.

Association for Supervision and Curriculum Development. (1994). *Understanding the Conflict over Outcome-Based Education* (audiotape). Alexandria, Va.: author.

Astuto, T.A., D.L. Clark, A. Read, K. McGree, L. de Koven, and P. Fernandez. (1994). *Roots of Reform: Challenging the Assumptions That Control Change in Education*. Bloomington: Phi Delta Kappa.

Atwell, N. (1987). *In the Middle: Writing, Reading, and Learning with Adolescents*. Portsmouth, N.H.: Boynton/Cook.

Bamburg, J., and E. Medina. (1993). "Analyzing Student Achievement: Using Standardized Tests as the First Step." In *Assessment: How Do We Know What They Know?* edited by J. Bamburg. Dubuque: Kendall-Hunt.

Berrueta-Clement, J.R. (1984). *Changed Lives*. Ypsilanti, Mich.: High Scope.

Bishop, J.H. (June 1995). "Improving Education: How Large Are the Benefits?" Written testimony delivered before a U.S. Senate Subcommittee on September 2, 1995. *Network News and Views*: 21–37.

Blase, J.L. (1986). "A Qualitative Analysis of Teacher Stress: Consequences for Performance." *American Educational Research Journal* 23: 13–40.

Blase, J., and P.C. Kirby. (December 1992). "The Power of Praise—A Strategy for Effective Principals." *NASSP Bulletin* 76, 548: 69–77.

Brigham, S.E. (1994). "TQM: Lessons We Can Learn from Industry." Anthologized in *Quality Goes to School*. Arlington, Va.: American Association of School Administrators.

Brooks, J.G., and M.G. Brooks. (1993). *The Case for Constructivist Classrooms*. Alexandria, Va.: Association for Supervision and Curriculum Development.

Bullard, P., and B.O. Taylor. (1993). *Making School Reform Happen*. New York: Allyn and Bacon.

Byham, W.C. (1992). *Zapp! in Education*. New York: Fawcett Columbine.

Caine, R.N., and G. Caine. (1991). *Making Connections: Teaching and the Human Brain*. Alexandria, Va.: Association for Supervision and Curriculum Development.

Carbo, M. (1986). *Teaching Students to Read Through Their Individual Learning Styles*. Englewood Cliffs, N.J.: Prentice-Hall.

Carnine, D. (December 8, 1993). "Facts Over Fads." *Education Week* 13, 14: 40.

Chang, Y.S., G. Labovitz, and V. Rosansky. (1992). *Making Quality Work: A Leadership Guide for the Results-Driven Manager*. Essex Junction, Vt.: Omneo.

112   Clark, D., S. Lotto, and T. Astuto. (1984). "Effective Schools and School Improvement: A Comparative Analysis of Two Lines of Inquiry." *Educational Administration Quarterly* 20, 3: 41–68.

Clarridge, P.B., and E.M. Whitaker. (October 1994). "Implementing a New Elementary Progress Report." *Educational Leadership* 52, 2: 7–9.

Cookson, P.W. (1985). *Preparing for Power: America's Elite Boarding Schools.* New York: Basic Books.

Csikszentmihalyi, M. (1990). *Flow: The Psychology of Optimal Experience.* New York: Harper Perennial.

Daggett, W. (June 1994). "Today's Students, Yesterday's Schooling." *The Executive Educator* 16, 6: 18–21.

Daniel, L. (1993). "Aligning Curriculum, Instruction and Assessment for a K–12 Writing Program." In *Assessment: How Do We Know What They Know?* edited by J. Bamburg. Dubuque: Kendall/Hunt.

Darling-Hammond, L., and A.L. Goodwin. (1993). "Progress Toward Professionalism in Teaching." In *Challenges and Achievements of American Education* (The 1993 ASCD Yearbook), edited by G. Cawelti. Alexandria, Va.: Association for Supervision and Curriculum Development.

David, J. (May 1994). "School-Based Decision-Making: Kentucky's Test of Decentralized Decision Making." *Phi Delta Kappan* 75, 9: 706–712.

Deming, W.E. (1986). *Out of the Crisis.* Cambridge: MIT Press.

Donahoe, T. (December 1993). "Finding the Way: Structure, Time, and Culture in School Improvement." *Phi Delta Kappan* 75, 4: 298–305.

DuFour, R. (April 1995). "Restructuring Is Not Enough." *Educational Leadership* 52, 7: 33–36.

Edmonds, R. (October 1979). "Effective Schools for the Urban Poor." *Educational Leadership* 37, 1: 15–24.

ERS Bulletin. (December 1990). "Biology Education," p. 4.

Evans, K.M., and J.A. King. (March 1994). "Research on OBE: What We Know and Don't Know." *Educational Leadership* 51, 6: 12.

Evans, R. (May 1989). "The Faculty in Midcareer: Implications for School Improvement." *Educational Leadership* 46, 8: 10–15.

Evans, R. (September 1993). "The Human Face of Reform." *Educational Leadership* 51, 1: 19–23.

Fiske, E.B. (1992). *Smart Schools, Smart Kids: Why Do Some Schools Work?* New York: Touchstone.

Folzenlogen, P. Speaker at *Fortune Magazine* Education Summit, Washington, D.C., Sept. 23, 1993.

Frankl, V.E. (1963). *Man's Search for Meaning: An Introduction to Logotherapy.* New York: Pocket Books.

Fullan, M. (1993). "Innovation, Reform and Restructuring Strategies." In *Challenges and Achievements of American Education* (The 1993 ASCD Yearbook), edited by G. Cawelti. Alexandria, Va.: Association for Supervision and Curriculum Development.

Fullan, M. (1994). "Teacher Leadership: A Failure To Conceptualize." In *Teachers as Leaders: Perspectives on the Professional Development of Teachers,* edited by D. Walling. Bloomington: Phi Delta Kappa.

Fullan, M.G., with S. Stiegelbauer. (1991). *The New Meaning of Educational Change.* New York: Teachers College Press.

Fullan, M.G., and M.B. Miles. (June 1992). "Getting Reform Right. What Works and What Doesn't?" *Phi Delta Kappan* 73, 10: 745–752.

Gamoran, A., and M. Nystrand. (1992). "Taking Students Seriously." In *Student Engagement and Achievement in American Secondary Schools*, edited by F.M. Newmann. New York: Teachers College Press.

Gardner, H., and V. Boix-Mansilla. (February 1994). "Teaching for Under-standing—Within and Across the Disciplines." *Educational Leadership* 51, 5: 14–18.

Gitlin, A. (Summer 1990)."Understanding Teaching Dialogically." *Teachers College Record* 91, 4: 537–563.

Glickman, C.D. (May 1991). "Pretending Not to Know What We Know." *Educational Leadership* 48, 8: 4–10.

Glickman, C.D. (1993). *Renewing America's Schools: A Guide for School-Based Action*. San Francisco: Jossey-Bass.

Goodlad, J.I. (November 1975). "Schools Can Make a Difference." *Educational Leadership* 33, 2: 108–117.

Goodlad, J.I. (1984). *A Place Called School*. New York: McGraw-Hill.

Goodlad, J.I. , M.F. Klein, and Associates. (1970). *Behind the Classroom Door*. Worthington, Ohio: Charles A. Jones.

Greene, B., and S. Uroff. (February 1989). "Apollo High School: Achievement Through Self-Esteem." *Educational Leadership* 46, 2: 80–81.

Guskey, T.R. (March 1994). "What You Assess May *Not* Be What You Get." *Educational Leadership* 51, 6: 51–54.

Guthrie, J.W. (March 1993). "Do America's Schools Need a 'Dow Jones Index'?" *Phi Delta Kappan* 74, 7: 523.

Haberman, M. (December 1990). "The Pedagogy of Poverty Versus Good Teaching." *Phi Delta Kappan* 73, 4: 290–294.

Haladyna, T.M., S.B. Nolen, and N. Haas. (June–July 1991). "Raising Stand-ardized Achievement Test Scores and the Origins of Test Score Pollution." *Educational Researcher* 20, 5: 2–7.

Hartmann, J.A., E.K. DeCicco, and G. Griffin. (November 1994). "Urban Students Thrive as Independent Researchers." *Educational Leadership* 52, 3: 46–47.

Hillocks, G., Jr. (May 1987). "Synthesis of Research on Teaching Writing." *Educational Leadership* 44, 8: 71–82.

Hodges, H. (March 1987). "I Know They Can Learn Because I've Taught Them." *Educational Leadership* 44, 6: 3.

Hopfenberg, W.S., H. Levin, G. Meister, and J. Roers. (1990). "Accelerated Schools." Accelerated Schools Project paper, Stanford University.

Hopkins, D. (1993). *A Teacher's Guide to Classroom Research*. Buckingham: Open University Press.

Hopkins, D., and M. West. (1994). "Teacher Development and School Im-provement: An Account of the Improving the Quality of Education for All (IQEA) Project." In *Teachers as Leaders: Perspectives on the Professional Development of Teachers*, edited by D. Walling. Bloomington: Phi Delta Kappa.

Howe, H., II, and M. Vickers. (July 14, 1993). "Standards and Diversity Down Under." *Education Week* 12, 39: 36.

Jaeger, R.M., B.E. Gorney, and R.L. Johnson. (October 1994). "The *Other* Kind of Report Card: When Schools Are Graded." *Educational Leadership* 52, 2: 42–45.

114 Jones, R. (April 1995). "Writing Wrongs." *The Executive Educator* 17, 4: 18–24.

Joyce, B., J. Wolf, and E. Calhoun. (1993). *The Self-Renewing School*. Alexandria, Va.: Association for Supervision and Curriculum Development.

Katzenbach, J.R., and D.K. Smith. (1993). *The Wisdom of Teams*. New York: Harper Business.

Kohn, A. (September 1993). "Turning Learning into a Business: Concerns About Total Quality." *Educational Leadership* 51, 1: 58–61.

Krashen, S. (1993). *The Power of Reading*. Englewood, Colo.: Libraries Unlimited.

Lickona, T. (1991). *Educating for Character*. New York: Bantam.

Little, J.W. (1987). "Teachers as Colleagues." In *Educator's Handbook*, edited by V. Richardson-Koehler. White Plains: Longman.

Little, J.W. (Summer 1990). "The Persistence of Privacy: Autonomy and Initiative in Teachers' Professional Relations." *Teachers College Record* 91, 4: 509–536.

Livingston, C., S. Castle, and J. Nations. (April 1989). "Testing and Curriculum Reform: One School's Experience." *Educational Leadership* 46, 7: 23–25.

Lortie, D.C. (1975). *Schoolteacher: A Sociological Study*. Chicago: University of Chicago Press.

Lounsbury, J.H., and D.C. Clark. (1990). *Inside Grade Eight: From Apathy to Excitement*. Reston, Va.: National Association of Secondary School Principals.

Maeroff, G.I. (March 1993). "Building Teams to Rebuild Schools." *Phi Delta Kappan* 74, 7: 512–519.

Maeroff, G.I. (1994). "On Matters of Body and Mind: Overcoming Disincentives to a Teaching Career." In *Teachers as Leaders: Perspectives on the Professional Development of Teachers*, edited by D. Walling. Bloomington: Phi Delta Kappa.

Malen, B., R.T. Ogawa, and J. Kranz. (February 1990). "Site-Based Management: Unfulfilled Promises." *School Administrator* 47, 2: 30–59.

Marzano, R.J., and S. Arthur. (1977). "Teacher Comments on Student Essays: It Doesn't Matter What You Say." University of Colorado, Denver: ERIC ED 147864.

Marzano, R.J., D. Pickering, and J. McTighe. (1993). *Assessing Student Outcomes*. Alexandria, Va.: Association for Supervision and Curriculum Development.

McDonald, J.P. (1993). "Planning Backwards from Exhibitions." In *Graduation by Exhibition: Assessing Genuine Achievement*, by J. McDonald, E. Barton, S. Smith, D. Turner, and M. Finney. Alexandria, Va.: Association for Supervision and Curriculum Development.

McGonagill, G. (1992). "Overcoming Barriers to Educational Restructuring: A Call for 'System Literacy.'" ERIC, ED 357512.

McPherson, G.H. (1972). *Small Town Teacher*. Cambridge: Harvard University Press.

Means, B., C. Chelemer, and M. Knapp, eds. (1991). *Teaching Advanced Skills to At-Risk Students*. San Francisco: Jossey-Bass.

Mortimore, P., and P. Sammons. (September 1987). "New Evidence on Effective Elementary Schools." *Educational Leadership* 45, 1: 4–8.

Muncey, D., and P.J. McQuillan. (February 1993). "Preliminary Findings from a 5-Year Study of the Coalition of Essential Schools." *Phi Delta Kappan* 74, 6: 486–489.

Murphy, J.A. (October 1988). "Improving the Achievement of Minority Students." *Educational Leadership* 46, 2: 41–42.

National Council of Teachers of Mathematics (NCTM). (February 1994). *Algebra for Everyone* (a brief statement distributed to members). Reston, Va.: author.

Newmann, F.M., ed. (1992). *Student Engagement and Achievement in American Secondary Schools*. New York: Teachers College Press.

Odden, A., D. Monk, Y. Nakib, and L. Picus. (October 1995). "The Story of the Education Dollar: No Academy Awards and No Smoking Guns." *Phi Delta Kappan* 77, 2: 161–168.

Olson, L. (June 15, 1994a). "Writing Still Needs Work, Report Finds." *Education Week* 13, 38: 1.

Olson, L. (June 22, 1994b). "International Math and Science Study Finds U.S. Covers More in Less Depth." *Education Week* 13, 39: 10.

O'Neil, J. (September 1992). "Science Education: Schools Pushed to Broaden Access, Overhaul Practice." *ASCD Curriculum Update*: 1–5.

O'Neil, J. (March 1993). "Achievement of U.S. Students Debated." *ASCD Update* 35, 3: 1, 3–5.

O'Neil, J. (August 1994). "Making Assessment Meaningful." *ASCD Update* 36, 6: 1, 4–5.

Osborne, D., and T. Gaebler. (1992). *Reinventing Government: How the Entrepreneurial Spirit Is Transforming the Public Sector*. New York: Addison Wesley.

Palincsar, A.S., and L.J. Klenk. (1991). "Dialogues Promoting Reading Comprehension." In *Teaching Advanced Skills to At-Risk Students*, edited by B. Means, C. Chelemer, and M. Knapp. San Francisco: Jossey-Bass.

Parker, W.C. (1991). *Renewing the Social Studies Curriculum*. Alexandria, Va.: Association for Supervision and Curriculum Development.

Peters, T. (1987). *Thriving on Chaos*. New York: Alfred A. Knopf.

Peters, T., and R. Waterman. (1982). *In Search of Excellence*. New York: Harper and Row.

Peterson, D. (1991). *A Better Idea*. Boston: Houghton Mifflin.

Pikulski, J.H. (September 1994). "Preventing Reading Failure: A Review of Five Effective Programs." *The Reading Teacher* 48, 1: 17, 30–39.

Pogrow, S. (April 1988). "Teaching Thinking to At-Risk Elementary Students." *Educational Leadership* 45, 7: 79–85.

Pogrow, S. (February 1990). "A Socratic Approach to Using Computers with At-Risk Students." *Educational Leadership* 47, 5: 61–66.

Reich, R.B. (1992). *The Work of Nations*. New York: Vintage.

Resnick, L.B., V.L. Bill, S.B. Lesgold, and M.N. Leer. (1991). "Thinking in Arithmetic Class." In *Teaching Advanced Skills to At-Risk Students*, edited by B. Means, C. Chelemer, and M. Knapp. San Francisco: Jossey-Bass.

Rosenholtz, S. (March 1989). "Workplace Conditions That Affect Teacher Quality and Commitment: Implications for Teacher Induction Programs." *The Elementary School Journal* 89, 4: 421–439.

116

Rosenholtz, S.J. (1991). *Teacher's Workplace: The Social Organization of Schools.* New York: Teachers College Press.

Rothman, R. (April 1, 1992a). "Science Reform Goals Elusive, NAEP Data Find." *Education Week* 11, 28: 15.

Rothman, R. (April 22, 1992b). "In a Pilot Study, Writing is Gauged." *Education Week* 11, 31: 24.

Sarason, S.B. (1982). *The Culture of the School and the Problem of Change.* Boston: Allyn and Bacon.

Schaffer, R.C., and H. Thomson. (January–February 1992). "Successful Change Programs Begin with Results." *Harvard Business Review* 70, 1: 80–92.

Schaffer, R.H. (1988). *The Breakthrough Strategy: Using Short-Term Successes to Build the High-Performance Organization.* New York: Harper Business.

Schmoker, M.J., and R. Wilson. (1993). *Total Quality Education: Profiles of Schools That Demonstrate the Power of Deming's Management Principles.* Bloomington: Phi Delta Kappa.

Secretary's Commission on Achieving Necessary Skills (SCANS). (1992). *SCANS Report.* Washington, D.C.: U.S. Department of Labor.

Senge, P. (1990). *The Fifth Discipline: The Art and Practice of the Learning Organization.* New York: Doubleday.

Shanker, A. (April 4, 1994). American Federation of Teachers Advertisement. *The New Republic,* p. 43.

Shavelson, R.J., and G.P. Baxter. (May 1992). "What We've Learned About Assessing Hands-On Science." *Educational Leadership* 49, 8: 20–25.

Sizer, T.R. (1992). *Horace's School: Redesigning the American High School.* New York: Houghton Mifflin.

Slavin, R.E., N.A. Madden, L.J. Dolan, B.A. Wasik, S.M. Ross, and L.J. Smith. (April 1994). "Whenever and Wherever We Choose: The Replication of Success for All." *Phi Delta Kappan* 75, 8: 639–647.

Smith, M. (June–July 1991). "Put to the Test: The Effects of External Testing on Teachers." *Educational Researcher* 20, 5: 8–11.

Smith, P. (1985). *America Enters the World.* New York: McGraw-Hill.

Smith, P. (1987). *Redeeming the Time: A People's History of the 1920s and the New Deal.* New York: McGraw-Hill.

Smith, W.F., and R.L. Andrews. (1989). *Instructional Leadership: How Principals Make a Difference.* Alexandria, Va.: Association for Supervision and Curriculum Development.

Steele, C.M. (April 1992). "Race and Schooling of Black Americans." *Atlantic Monthly,* p. 75.

Stiggins, R.J. (1994). *Student-Centered Classroom Assessment.* New York: Merrill.

Thoreau, H.D. (1946). *Walden, or Life in the Woods.* New York: Bodd, Mead.

Turner, D., and M. Finney. (1993). "The MultiMedia Exhibition." In *Graduation by Exhibition: Assessing Genuine Achievement,* by J. McDonald, S. Smith, D. Turner, M. Finney, and E. Barton. Alexandria, Va.: Association for Supervision and Curriculum Development.

Viadero, D. (February 9, 1994). "Impact of Reform Said to Be Spotty and Not Systemic." *Education Week* 13, 20: 1.

Walberg, H.J., G.D. Haertel, and S. Gerlach-Downie. (1994). *Assessment Reform: Challenges and Opportunities.* Bloomington: Phi Delta Kappa.

Walton, M. (1986). *The Deming Management Method.* New York: Perigee.
Walton, M. (1990). *Deming Management at Work.* New York: Perigee.
Waters, T., D. Burger, and S. Burger. (March 1995). "Moving up Before Moving on." *Educational Leadership* 52, 6: 35–40.
West, P. (April 1, 1992). "Math Teachers' Survey Finds a Schism Between Practice, Reformer's Vision." *Education Week* 11, 28: 1.
West, P. (December 8, 1994). "Efficacy of U.S. Aid for Science, Math Questioned." *Education Week* 14, 14: 1.
Wheatley, M. (1994). *Leadership and the New Science.* San Francisco: Berrett-Koehler.
Wiggins, G. (1993). *Standards, NOT Standardization.* Center on Learning Assessment and School Structure. Geneseo, N.Y.: Greater Insights Productions.
Wiggins, G. (July 1994a). "None of the Above." *The Executive Educator* 16, 7: 14–18.
Wiggins, G. (October 1994b). "Toward Better Report Cards." *Educational Leadership* 52, 2: 28–37.
Wolfe, P., and M. Sorgen. (1990). *Mind, Memory and Learning: Implications for the Classroom.* Fairfax, Va.: Patricia Wolfe and Marny Sorgen.

Index

A

accelerated schools, 32, 78
accountability
    and professionalism, 48
    and test scores, 3
    difficulty in showing, 70
    in OBE movement, 34
    nonthreatening, 36
    reasonable, 47
    to community, 47, 48
    with results-orientation, 79
Adlai E. Stevenson High School, Lincoln-
    shire, Ill., 15–16
affective measures, 98–100
African American students, 50
algebra, 50, 85–86. *See also* math
Algebra for Everyone, 85
Allied Signal Corp., Tucson, Ariz., 41
alternative programs, 43–44
American Federation of Teachers, 55
Amphitheater High School, Tucson, Ariz.,
    52, 73, 91–92
Amphitheater Middle School, Tucson,
    Ariz., 50
Amphitheater School District, Tucson,
    Ariz., 47, 60, 96, 109
anchor papers, 75, 76, 95
Ann Arbor, Mich., public schools, 95, 100
anonymity
    for reporting results, 24, 85
    in compiling results, 87
    in selecting data, 35
Apollo High School, Simi Valley, Calif., 43
Assessing Student Outcomes, 72, 84
assessments. *See also* report cards; rubrics;
    standardized tests
    alternative, in science, 86–87
    as goals, 24
    Australian, 83
    essay exams, 74
    frequent, 88–90

assessments *(continued)*
    in Pomperaug Regional School Dis-
      trict, 43, 44, 88–89
    reporting, 79
    sample social studies, 82
    sharing, 102
at-risk students, 21, 78
Atwell, Nancie, 44
Australian graduation exams, 83
authentic learning, 17
autonomy in selecting data, 35, 87

B

Beck, Rosemary, 109
behavior. *See* student responsibility and be-
    havior; student social behavior and char-
    acter development
benefits
    of rubrics, 71–72
    of teamwork, 11–13
    psychological, of short-term results, 57
Bent, Bill, 109
Bradley Commission, 83
brain research, need for applying, 66

C

California Achievement Test, 20. *See also*
    standardized tests
Canyon Del Oro High School, Tucson,
    Ariz., 99
Castner, Kevin, 4, 28
Centennial Elementary School, Evans,
    Colo., 23–24, 36, 42, 60
Central Park East Secondary School, New
    York City, N.Y., 43, 78
Champlain Valley High School,
    Burlington, Vt., 97
Champlin, John, 50
Chapter I students, 17, 40–41
Christensen, Dolores, 91
class cutting, 42, 50

Clovis, Calif., public schools, 47, 100
Coalition of Essential Schools, 55, 78, 93
community, accountability to, 47, 48
computers, 42, 76, 110
cooperative learning, 4–5, 24, 25

D
Daniel Webster School, San Francisco,
Calif., 78
Deming, W. Edwards, 12, 13, 23, 28, 51
Detroit, Mich., public schools, 78
discussion skills, 93–94
Dodge Park Elementary School, Prince
George's County, Md., 20
Domino Sugar Co., 59
Donaldson Elementary School, Tucson,
Ariz., 11, 40
Dotts, Wayne, 94
DuFour, Richard, 15

E
early-intervention programs, 41, 51, 67,
94–95
early-outs, 11, 16
Edison, Thomas, 9
education literature, 26, 56, 61
Elvira Elementary School, Tucson, Ariz., 78
enthusiasm. *See* student enthusiasm
Escalante, Jaime, 43
exemplary work, need for, 75–76

F
Farmer, Noel, 17
fear
of data and results, 33–34
reducing, from data and goal-setting,
34–36
feedback
as antidote for fatalism in schools, 45
from rubrics, 71, 72
from specific goals, 23
interchangeable with data, 30
psychological need for, 57
synonymous with results, 3
Fitzpatrick, James, 97
Fort Pitt Elementary School, Pittsburgh,
Pa., 44–45, 50
Frankl, Viktor, 19
Frederick County, Md., public schools, 17,
101, 102, 105

G
Gardner, Howard, 79, 81
George Westinghouse Vocational and
Technical School, Brooklyn, N.Y., 42, 50
Gilbert High School, Gilbert, Ariz., 91
Glickman, Carl, 24–25, 27, 32, 34, 108
GM-Toyota NUMMI plant, Calif., 41

H
happiness, 18. *See also* student enthusiasm
Hawthorne Elementary School, Seattle,
Wash., 50
Hendery, Dan, 88
Henry Levin schools, 31
Hess, Steve, 81, 101
Hibbard, Michael, 89
Higher-Order Thinking Skills (HOTS) pro-
gram, 78
Holaway Elementary School, Tucson,
Ariz., 15, 88
Hollibrook Elementary School, Houston,
Tx., 32, 78, 99
*Horace's School: Redesigning the American
High School,* 89
HOTS program. *See* Higher-Order Think-
ing Skills (HOTS) program

I
Iaccoca, Lee, 59
impatience in results-driven programs,
56–57
Individual Education Plans (IEPs), 37
innovations
compared to objectives, 25
how school culture affects, 22
impact on student learning, 26
implementing, 2
isolation of teachers preventing, 12
monitoring impact of, 5
In Search of Excellence, 47
intellectual capital, 12, 15
interdisciplinary results. *See* discussion
skills; oral presentations; reading

J
James Comer schools, 31
Johnson City High School, N.Y., 88
Johnson City School District, N.Y., 6, 44, 50
Joiner, Brian, 56
Junior Great Books Foundation, 93

120

K

Keeling Elementary School, Tucson, Ariz., 97
Key School, New York City, N.Y., 8, 79, 91
Kohn, Alfie, 30
Kyrene School District, Tempe, Ariz., 80, 90

L

La Cima Middle School, Tucson, Ariz., 42, 50, 87, 97
language arts and literature, 84
late-ins, 16
leadership
    emphasis on common goals, 104
    for nationwide improvement, 108
    influence on school culture, 105, 107
    need for improvement in, 53
    recognition of teacher improvement efforts, 103–106
    research on, 67
    support for group data, 37
Lezotte, Larry, 77
literature. *See* education literature
low-achieving students
    in early-intervention programs, 95
    influence of socioeconomic factors on, 67–68
    need for applying research about, 66
    need for more data on, 40
    raising achievement of, 29–30
    rapid improvement of, 50, 54

M

Maryland Assessment Consortium, 45, 81
math, 15, 50, 53, 78, 85–86, 90
McTighe, Jay, 45
meetings, 13, 109–110
Meier, Deborah, 78
Mesa Verde Elementary School, Tucson, Ariz., 36, 39
Metropolitan Achievement Test, 45. *See also* standardized tests
Metropolitan Writing Exam, 50. *See also* standardized tests; writing
minority students, 20, 50

N

Nash Elementary School, Tucson, Ariz., 96, 97

National Council of Teachers of Mathematics (NCTM), 53, 85–86
National Geographic Society, 83
National History Standards Project, 82
New York Regents exam, 88
North Carolina Project, 45, 50, 100
Northview Elementary School, Manhattan, Kan., 14–15

O

Oak Harbor School District, Wash., 75
OBE. *See* outcomes-based education (OBE) movement
oral presentations, 91–93. *See also* discussion skills
outcomes. *See also* outcomes-based education (OBE) movement
    concern for, 5–6
    confused with processes, 58
    generalized, for evaluating students, 37
    influencing variables that affect, 40
    in productive meetings, 109
    teacher vulnerability from, 27–28
outcomes-based education (OBE) movement, 6, 34, 35, 46

P

Paideia Program, 93
parents
    accountability to, 47, 70
    and report cards, 80, 95
    and rubrics, 71, 74
    interest in exemplary work, 75–76
passive activities, 40, 53, 99
Peterson, Donald, 11
Pomperaug Regional School District 15, Conn., 43, 71, 83, 87, 88, 102
portfolios, 24, 87
Potter, Chris, 109
poverty, failure to reach children in, 53–54
presentism, 10
professionalism, 48
profit motive, 27
Prince Elementary School, Tucson, Ariz., 12
programs, 57–58. *See also* alternative programs; early-intervention programs; impatience in results-driven programs; Paideia Program

R

reading. 14, 78, 84, 94–96. *See also* early-intervention programs

Reading Recovery program, 51, 67, 94

Reading Renaissance program, 67, 94

Reinventing Government: How the Entrepreneurial Spirit Is Transforming the Public Sector, 27

report cards. *See also* assessments

  improving, 69

  indicators on, 80, 90, 95, 100

  redesigning, 79–80

research

  need for formal and local, 65

  opportunities for applying, 66–68

  role of, 64

  role of data in, 45–46

  underuse of formal, 2, 65–66

research papers, 96–97. *See also* writing

Rose, John, 47

rubrics, 31, 60, 70–79

  for discussion skills, 94

  for oral presentations, 91

  for reading, 84

  for responsibility, 97–98

  for writing, 73, 74–75

  in math, 15, 85, 88

  in science, 87

S

school culture, 105, 107–108

school reforms, 26–27, 31, 55–56

schools. *See names of specific schools*

science, 45, 52–53, 86–87

Senge, Peter, 6, 27, 42

Shanker, Al, 55

site-based management, 2, 4–5, 26–27, 58–59

social studies, 72, 79, 82–84

Sparks, Richard, 100

spirit of organizations, 106–107

staff development, 2, 25, 40

  budgeting, 53, 54

  cynicism about, 31

  teamwork as, 12, 85

Stand and Deliver (movie), 43

standardized tests. *See also* assessments; tests, objective

  relying on, 31

  supplementing, 3, 69, 70, 76–79

Standards, NOT Standardization, 72

statistics, 8, 41, 86

Still, Suzanne, 32

student enthusiasm, 13, 36, 45, 91

student responsibility and behavior, 97–98

student social behavior and character development, 100–101

subject areas. *See* language arts and literature; math; science; social studies

Success for All program, 41, 51, 67, 94–95

systemic change, 59–60

T

technology, 76. *See also* computers

tests, objective, 74. *See also* standardized tests

Texas Scholars Program, 8

Total Quality Management (TQM) movement, 4, 56–57

  at Centennial Elementary School, 24

  in industry, 5, 41

Toyota plant, Georgetown, Kent., 5, 13

Tucson, Ariz., Unified School District, 80

U

University of California, Berkeley, Calif., 50

V

Valley Oak Elementary School, Clovis, Calif., 100

W

Walbrook High School, Baltimore, Md., 91–92

Walther, Bill, 87

Weld County School District 6, 29–30, 75, 90

Westwood School, Dalton, Ga., 77

whole language instruction, 4–5, 24, 25

Wiggins, Grant, 4, 31, 32, 45, 76, 79

Wilson, Richard, 61, 63, 105, 106

The Wisdom of Teams, 12

writing, 30, 44, 66–67. *See also* research papers; rubrics, for writing

  improvement at specific schools, 8, 11, 24, 39, 44, 50, 52, 60

Y

Yunk, Dan, 15